The
EVERYTHING®
Drums Book

Dear Reader:

Welcome to *The Everything® Drums Book*! If you want to learn to play the drums, but don't know where to begin, look no further. This text is a comprehensive guide that will teach you a step-by-step approach to drumming.

Contrary to popular belief, playing the drums is no easy task. You can't just sit down at a drum set and whale away like a pro. Like any instrument, drumming requires a lot of dedication and hard work. The good news is that you can play the drums no matter what your age, and no matter what your musical background. Music has no restrictions; anybody can learn given the right educational tools and the proper motivation.

What you put in is what you get out. If you spend even a little time each day going through this book and practicing the various exercises found in each chapter, you will find that drumming is not only enjoyable, it is very rewarding.

By learning to play the drums, you will learn a great deal about who you are. This is the gift of music. Hopefully, this book will help you to tap into your creative side and to learn a little bit about what could be called "the great conversation" of music.

Notes on a page are and always will be silent. It's the individual that sets them to music. Don't be notes; be a song.

Thanks for reading,

Eric Alan

The EVERYTHING® Series

Editorial

Publishing Director	Gary M. Krebs
Managing Editor	Kate McBride
Copy Chief	Laura MacLaughlin
Acquisitions Editor	Eric Hall
Development Editor	Michael Paydos
Production Editor	Khrysti Nazzaro

Production

Production Director	Susan Beale
Production Manager	Michelle Roy Kelly
Series Designers	Daria Perreault
	Colleen Cunningham
Cover Design	Paul Beatrice
	Frank Rivera
Layout and Graphics	Colleen Cunningham
	Rachael Eiben
	Michelle Roy Kelly
	Daria Perreault
	Erin Ring
Cover Artist:	Dave Winter
Audio Production:	Nelson Starr
Music Typesetting:	Marc Schonbrun
Photography:	Jeffrey Starr
Additional Art:	Barry Littmann

Visit the entire Everything® Series at everything.com

THE
EVERYTHING®
DRUMS
BOOK

From tuning and timing to fills and
solos—all you need to keep the beat

Eric Starr

Adams Media Corporation
Avon, Massachusetts

In memory of Don Atkinson

_____

An Everything® Series Book.
Everything® and everything.com® are registered trademarks of F+W Publications, Inc.

Published by Adams Media, an F+W Publications Company
57 Littlefield Street, Avon, MA 02322 U.S.A.
www.adamsmedia.com

ISBN: 1-58062-886-9

Printed in the United States of America.

J I H G F E D C B

Library of Congress Cataloging-in-Publication Data
Starr, Eric.
The everything drums book / Eric Starr.
p.   cm.   (An everything series book)
Includes discography (p.   ).
ISBN 1-58062-886-9
1. Percussion instruments–Instruction and study. I. Title.
II. Series: Everything series.
MT655.S73 2003
786.9'193—dc21
2003001928

This publication is designed to provide accurate and authoritative information with regard to the subject matter covered. It is sold with the understanding that the publisher is not engaged in rendering legal, accounting, or other professional advice. If legal advice or other expert assistance is required, the services of a competent professional person should be sought.
—From a *Declaration of Principles* jointly adopted by a Committee of the American Bar Association and a Committee of Publishers and Associations

Many of the designations used by manufacturers and sellers to distinguish their products are claimed as trademarks. Where those designations appear in this book and Adams Media was aware of a trademark claim, the designations have been printed with initial capital letters.

This book is available at quantity discounts for bulk purchases.
For information, call 1-800-872-5627.

Contents

Acknowledgments

Thanks to all my teachers past and present, to Dave Meyers for his knowledge of Latin music, Mark Norris for his knowledge of rock history, and to Marc Schonbrun for his cogency and computer acumen. Also, a big thanks to my brothers Nelson and Jeffrey and to my patient wife Katherine (Rin). Special thanks to my parents and to my late grandparents, Charles and Ruth Freeman.

Recording

Audio engineered, mixed, and edited by Nelson M. Starr at Gardenwood Studios. All performances by Eric Starr.

Top Ten Reasons
to Take Up Drumming

1. No one can rock out like a drummer.

2. Schlepping your gear from gig to gig is cheaper than a membership to a gym, and it is an even better workout.

3. Percussion is a vital element of every musical style—from rock and blues to R & B to Caribbean.

4. Good drumming has always been the hallmark of hit songs.

5. You have always had great rhythm and musical interest, and now you want to put it to some good use.

6. Drumming will sharpen your concentration and hone your listening skills.

7. You don't need a Ph.D. in music theory to play the drums.

8. Drumming relieves stress and allows you to explore creative expression.

9. Practicing the drums will help you to develop your sense of time and reflexes.

10. Drummers are the heartbeat of any band.

Introduction

▶ DRUMS AND DRUMMING GO VERY FAR BACK into human history and have been used in virtually every major culture from Asia to the Americas, Africa to the Middle East. Drums unearthed from Mesopotamia date back to around 3000 B.C. Still other excavations around the world have produced drums twice this old.

In most early cultures, drums were used for both religious and civic purposes, and to this day, tribal and nontribal communities still use drums in religious rites or as accompaniment to everyday song and dance. North American, African, and Australian tribal communities all tell of drums in stories; this mythology is said to be thousands of years old.

If you go to a powwow anywhere in North America, you will hear Indians singing and dancing with percussive accompaniment. Powwows are mostly for recreation, but beyond the power lines, deep into Indian country, you will find Indians of various tribes using drums as a medium between worshippers and the spirit world. This has been going on since time immemorial.

As previously mentioned, drums are not only used in tribal culture. They are and have been a part of the Jewish, Christian, and Muslim religions for centuries. However, some religious groups—for instance, early Calvinists—feared that the drum would give rise to evil forces. This produced movements throughout history that saw the mass banning of music and drumming altogether. Fortunately, these movements did not last.

In Jewish history, we find references to the drum in the ancient Book of Maccabees. In the 1500s, Martin Luther, the father of the Protestant Reformation, recognized the power of music and specifically the drum. In ancient Islamic cultures, the beating of drums was used to publicly announce a marriage. These are but a few examples. Today, it's not hard to spot drums being used in all three major religions and in the secular music that has grown up around each culture.

Drums have also been used in the military for centuries. In fact, modern Western drumming techniques and rhythmical ideas are directly linked to this heritage. In the 1400s, the British and the Turks used drums and drummers to rally troops and to send messages across smoky battlefields. Earlier still, the Swiss Army used drums in the 1300s for these same reasons. As you will learn in Chapter 6, the military drumming tradition has been carried all the way through to modern times.

The drum set is quite modern, relatively speaking, anyway. In the early 1900s, New Orleans drummers began to group together drums with other accessories to create a variety of percussive tones and textures. This was originally called *double drumming*.

These drummers used instruments from the far reaches of the earth. For example, they used tom-toms and dragon mouths from the Orient, the latter being ornate wooden blocks. European bass drums and tenor drums were also employed, as were brass cymbals from Turkey. None of this would have occurred had New Orleans not been a vibrant port city and had there not been a large African-American population there, struggling to find an artistic voice in a racially prejudiced world.

By the 1920s, drum sets were becoming standard fare in jazz bands. However, it wasn't until the 1930s, and the dawn of the swing era, that the drum set became fully accepted in popular music. Still, it would take another decade or so before the drum set was to reach full maturity. Ⓔ

E How to Use This Book and CD

To get the most out of this book, we should talk about some of the notation and terms that will be used throughout this text. Some of it you have seen before; some of it may be new to you.

First Things First

Before we do anything, please familiarize yourself with the notation key below. Be sure to refer back to this often. For more information on notation, see Chapter 4.

KEY

BD=Bass Drum
FL=Floor Tom-tom
SN=Snare Drum
SS=Side Stick (clave sound)
T2=13" Rack Tom-tom
T1=12" Rack Tom-tom
HH/Ride=Hi-hat or Ride Cymbal
CR/SP=Crash Cymbal or Splash Cymbal

The Goal of *The Everything® Drums Book*

The primary goal of *The Everything® Drums Book* is not just to teach you how to play the drums, but rather, to teach you how to play music. You cannot play any instrument well unless you understand the full scope of music, an in-depth and interconnected art form. Therefore, this book is designed to help you better conceive of music as a cultural phenomena and way of life. In order to do this, you must learn how to channel feeling into musical expression. Music is a highly personalized act, and the quicker you understand this, the easier the learning process will be.

If you pick up the drumsticks and begin playing without any game plan or forethought, you will come up against a lot of roadblocks. In order to avoid this, you will be taught how to develop a perceptive, analytical musical mindset. This book leaves nothing to chance.

How You Can Use This Book

You can use this book in a variety of ways. If you're a beginner, it's best to follow the order as presented, chapter by chapter. By skipping around, you will miss valuable information and find that you become confused quickly. This book is set up cumulatively.

If you already have some academic knowledge of music and drumming, you may want to peruse the book for areas in your playing that need work. Maybe you never worked enough on your rudiments. Maybe you're not sure how to tune your drums. Maybe you don't know how to swing well in jazz. Whatever your deficiencies, you're sure to find easy-to-follow and credible information on a whole host of subjects.

The Everything® Drums Book covers a lot of ground. If you've always wanted to play the drums but didn't know where to start, this book is for you. All of the information and advice presented here can be applied in the real world. There is no filler or academic gibberish included on the following pages. Everything presented here is useful and practical. If you follow the musical path prescribed in this guide, you will be well on your way toward becoming a great drummer.

It's impossible to provide information about literally every aspect of drumming in one book. Given this, two appendices have been included in the back of the book for additional guidance and support.

Audio Examples

TRACK 1

As often as possible, the examples will be played on the audio CD that is included with this book. The examples are played at a moderate speed so you can hear the idea and also practice along with it. The examples that are on the CD will have this symbol next to the example number with a track number underneath it. These numbers correspond to tracks on the CD. The CD is a great tool that will help you unlock the more difficult examples and get them just right. Ⓔ

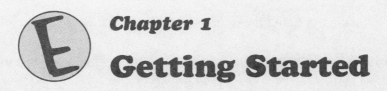

Chapter 1

Getting Started

Before you begin playing, you will need to prepare mentally for the job ahead. Also, since you will need to make a few purchases, you'll need to know the difference between quality instruments and poorly made ones. Finally, you will need to know how to set up and position your drums and/or practice pads. In brief, this chapter will give you the answers you need to start off correctly.

Mental Preparation

Before you pick up the sticks, it's important to cleanse your mind of any myths or other wrongheaded notions you may have about music. First of all, don't worry about becoming the best drummer in the world. Instead, focus on your budding relationship with music, and begin defining some basic objectives.

Start by asking yourself these questions:

- Would I like to become a professional or am I only interested in music as a hobby?
- Is there a particular style of music I would like to learn about? If so, what?
- Am I only interested in playing on a drum set or are there other percussion instruments I'd like to try?
- How committed am I to regular practice?

What other questions might you have? It's important that you begin developing a keen sense for music and drumming, and asking yourself questions will help you to become more focused. Keep in mind that you don't need to have every question answered immediately. All you need to do is start ruminating on them. Also, remember that your answers to many of these questions will change as the weeks, months, and years go by and your skills improve.

QUESTION?

Are you saying that spontaneity is bad?
There is nothing wrong with jamming or spontaneity. That's not the point. Certainly, there is an element to music that is born of surprise: from experimentation, mistakes, bursts of inspiration, and from just throwing caution to the wind and whacking those drums.

Each week, make a list of your musical goals and see how it evolves over time. When you play drums, or any instrument for that matter, you must first realize that everything you do should be deliberate and well conceived. Mindlessly flailing away on your drum set does you no good. In other words, if you don't think about what you're doing, your playing will reflect it.

Strong performances are mostly the result of training and mental discipline. You know you're a solid player when you have the ability to play what you *want* to play, rather than what just happens to come out. So for now, just concentrate on being deliberate and thoughtful in your practice. In the end, your jamming (or improvising) will be better for it. Why? You'll be in control, not your bad habits.

Keeping an Open Mind

The world is brimming with musical philosophies and there are many approaches to learning. One of the goals of *The Everything® Drums Book* is to help you get in touch with yourself and the way or ways you learn best. There is no one right way to do things. Similarly, there is no one wrong way either. Each person enters the musical arena with a different physiological and psychological makeup. Because of this, it is important to tailor your learning to best fit your needs.

Recognize that you are an individual with unique strengths and weaknesses. However, don't use this as an excuse to close yourself off from the world around you, to rationalize mediocrity, or make excuses to avoid learning the essentials of music making. Instead, use your individuality as a springboard for honest and thoughtful musical exploration.

If you reject ideas and concepts that seem foreign or even in conflict with your own, you will never improve. Instead, you will spiral down a dark path toward stubbornness and ignorance. Learning an instrument means that you must be an open receptacle for information and ideas. So, stay flexible, study the trails that have already been blazed, and heed the advice of those who have more experience than you.

Staying on Task

If you can't figure something out, or if you can't seem to play something the way you know it should be played, be patient and keep practicing. For many, frustration stands in the way of progress. However, this needn't be the case. Many students begin a task and conveniently set it aside because they tell themselves "I can't do it." Further, many students give up before they even begin. Don't let this be you. The truth is, you can accomplish anything you set your mind to if you plan appropriately, maintain a positive attitude, work diligently, and remain patient. Patience, and its close relative perseverance, is tantamount to success. So stay on task. Don't just skim through the exercises in this book, or try them once only to say "This is too hard" or "I can't do this." There will be snags along the way, but the frustration now will be the joy later.

FACT

Musical roadblocks will stand in your way, but don't avoid them. Recognize these obstacles as challenges and overcome them. This will bring you a feeling of fulfillment and accomplishment. Almost nothing worth doing is easy.

Buying the Right Drums and Cymbals

Some professionals contend that any drum can sound good, while others are extremely picky about what they will play on. For your purposes, just about any drum or cymbal that is in good condition will do. Use your ears when deciding. Does the drum or cymbal have a tone that is pleasing to you? If not, try something else. If it's a drum in question, ask the clerk at the store if it has been tuned recently. Often, even great drums sound lousy in stores because they are factory-direct or have not been tuned in months, or ever.

Who to Buy From

The most respected drum manufacturers today are Ludwig, Tama, Pearl, Yamaha, Drum Workshop (DW), Gretsch, Slingerland, Premier, Sonor, Noble & Cooley, and Remo. Ayotte and Peavey are companies on the rise, and there are vintage drums, such as Rogers and Leedy, still being sold today. Finally, Grover Pro Percussion makes high-end snare drums.

You can't go wrong with any of these companies. However, it's important to stay away from cheaply made plywood drums or overpriced, low-quality student model sets. If you're a smart consumer, you can find used semiprofessional (or even pro) drum sets made by the companies previously listed for almost the same price as many new student model sets!

Cymbals

The same applies for cymbals. Cymbals are tapered, circular brass plates that contain a small cup or bell that swells at the cymbal's center. Two cymbals stacked on top of each other and played both with the hands and with a foot pedal are called *hi-hats*. The big three cymbal manufacturers are Zildjian, Sabian, and Paiste. Zildjian is recognized as the oldest company in the world dating back to the 1600s; they also far outsell any other cymbal manufacturer.

However, this doesn't mean that Zildjian is the only quality cymbal company or even the best. Other companies such as Istanbul (Agop and Mehmet), Bosphorus, and Meinl make high-quality cymbals as well. Istanbul and Bosphorus offer genuine hand-hammered cymbals that are made exclusively in Turkey. Meinl offers a fine hand-hammered Turkish line of cymbals, too, although most of their models are manufactured in Germany. In general, Meinl can also be hard to find on American shores and some of their lines are not sold in the United States at all.

Meinl and Bosphorus are probably the least-recognized cymbal companies, but their reputations are growing and their product lines are as good as the big three companies, if not superior. In particular, Bosphorus's Master Series is absolutely exquisite, as is Meinl's Byzance Series. Meinl also makes fine hand percussion instruments.

The biggest problem with all cymbals these days is their cost. Again, as with drums, used cymbals may be your best bet. In fact, some professionals will *only* play on used cymbals because they have a warmer tone and don't need to be "broken in."

The Snare Drum

As a beginner, the snare drum is the main instrument you will be focusing on, and is the central instrument within the drum set. There are essentially two types of snare drums on the market: wooden-shelled drums and chrome-shelled drums. In rare cases, you may come across plastic- or composite-shelled drums, too. A common starter snare drum is a chrome 5½" × 14" eight-lug drum.

The snare drum contains:

- A shell or circular body
- A top "batter" head and a bottom ultra-thin clear head
- Chrome hoops (rims) that fasten the heads to the shell
- Tension rods that screw into lug casings (these are used to tighten the rim onto the shell)
- Snare wires
- A throw-off apparatus

Whatever drum you buy, make certain that the snare (thin metal strings on the bottom of the drum) are intact and that the throw-off lever on the side of the drum works properly. The throw-off is a chrome

FIGURE 1-1
Snare drum, top view

apparatus found on the side or shell of the snare drum. It contains a lever that snaps the snare wires up against the bottom drumhead or releases them so that they hang about ⅛" below the head. See **FIGURES 1-1** and **1-2**.

When the throw-off or strainer is in the up position, you will hear the buzz of the snare wires. When the throw-off is in the sideways position, the drum will sound similar to a high-pitched tom-tom. Tom-toms are similar to snare drums in that they have two heads fastened to a shell. They do not contain snare wires though. They also differ from the snare drum in their function. You will learn about the function of tom-toms in Chapters 14 and 15.

When checking the snare strainer, make sure that you can turn the snares on and off without too much effort. Also, make sure that the snares tighten and release quietly. If you do not get this on-off effect at all, it may simply mean that the snare wires are too loose.

FIGURE 1-2
Snare drum, bottom view

All quality snare drums have an adjustment knob that is part of the throw-off apparatus. If the snare is not working properly, try tightening this knob. You should feel the tension increase depending on the direction you turn it. If you turn the knob and it has no effect on the sound of the drum, chances are the apparatus is faulty. Don't buy this drum.

Finally—and this goes for any drum—check to see if the drum has any cracks in the shell and make sure that the rims or hoops that fasten the head to the shell are not bent or dented. Also, make sure that none of the tension rods (screws) are missing, and check that none of the lugs (tension rod casings) are stripped. Don't worry about heads, because these are dispensable. Often the head that comes with your purchase needs replacing anyway.

Once upon a time, drumheads were made from calf hides (skin). However, the problem with skins was that they were very difficult to keep in tune due to fluctuations in the weather. They were also not very durable. Nowadays, we use plastic or Mylar heads on our drums and the most popular head manufacturer is Remo, although Evans and Aquarian make fine heads, too.

On the bottom of your snare drum, you must use an ultra-thin clear head. Anything thicker will choke the snare wires and they will not vibrate. Also, you should use only a single-ply "batter" head on the top of your snare drum. The batter head is a rough, sandpapery-surfaced head that is designed to give texture to brush strokes. If the head were smooth, brushing the head would have little effect. The batter head is also single-ply to allow for a crisper tone and more sustain. The white Remo Ambassador Batter is the most common of its kind. You may use the Ambassador Batter heads on all of your drums. However, a heavier, double-ply pinstripe head is very popular with many drummers because of its durability and rounder tone on tom-toms. The pinstripe head rings less, and therefore has fewer overtones. Whatever you do, definitely use the pinstripe head for your bass drum, as this will give you the necessary punch and durability you need.

FACT

You will need to change your top or "batter" snare head every three to six months depending on your degree of activity.

In most cases, you don't need to replace the bottom tom-tom heads, front bass drumhead, and bottom snare head with high-quality heads since you will never strike these heads. Whatever heads come from the factory (or the person who had the drums before you) are probably good enough as long as there are no rips or holes in them. Professionals often search for the perfect head combinations, but you needn't worry about this. Concentrate on learning to play first.

Full Sets

If you purchase a full drum set, don't be concerned with getting a full array of tom-toms, cymbals, and other accessories. A simple four-piece (9" × 12" rack tom, 16" × 16" floor tom, and 15" × 22" bass drum) will suffice. Rack tom-toms are mounted on top of the bass drum; floor toms stand on the floor supported by three metal legs. The bass drum (also called a kick) is the largest drum in the kit and is played exclusively with your foot using a pedal; the pedal contains a felt beater that strikes the drum.

Many kits also come with a 10" × 13" rack tom as well. If you do buy a kit, you might as well go the distance, however, and include both a ride cymbal (20" to 22") and a crash cymbal (15" to 18") in your purchase. You'll learn the functions of these types of cymbals in Chapter 11. Also, don't forget the hi-hats (14") and stand, bass drum pedal, and padded throne or drum stool. Finally, for beginners, cases are optional since you will not be traveling all over town, night after night, with your gear. If you do buy cases, Humes & Berg makes easy to use nylon padded bags. They call them Tuxedo cases.

In summary, do not to be fooled by beautiful, sparkly new drums and cymbals, since this can be misleading. As you may have guessed by now, used drums and cymbals should not, in any way, be looked down upon. In fact, many in-the-know drummers enjoy scouting for rare and used equipment, and revel in stories of how they found some great snare drum or cymbal tucked away in the bargain bin at a pawn shop, tag sale, or even large retail outlet. So, take your time and find equipment that will keep you satisfied for at least a few years.

ALERT!

Climate control is essential to the health of your drums and cymbals. Extreme cold can cause shell veneers to peel off and/or crack. Consistent contact with moisture can also cause the brass on cymbals and the chrome on drums to rust.

Buying the Right Accessories

Buying the right gear is extremely important. Having the most expensive or fancy equipment is not. As you begin to define your goals and solidify your musical interests, you will be able to make better decisions about what drums, cymbals, hardware, sticks, pads, and other equipment you will want to use for practice. You may even begin to think about what your dream drum set might be. At this stage of the game, however, it is important not to become overly preoccupied with equipment. You will want to make smart purchases, but don't get caught up in a retail frenzy, or you will only waste your money.

Drum Pads

Drum pads are an essential part of every drummer's collection. Beginners often can't afford drums themselves, so pads take on even more relevance. As of this writing, the best pad on the market is the gum rubber Real Feel drum pad. This pad will give you the necessary bounce you need to develop good technique. The Remo Drum Company also makes fine pads and pad drum sets (though they are a little loud). If neither pad is available, ask the clerk at your local music store which pads offer great stick rebound and a quiet surface.

Since drums themselves can be very loud, the pad offers a wonderful alternative to supplying earplugs for your entire neighborhood. Do yourself a favor and make a pad and/or pad set your first purchase. Keep in mind that if you cannot afford an actual drum set, pads are a legitimate alternative. In other words, you can develop nearly all the techniques and skills needed to be a drummer with only pads; every serious drummer works out on pads at least part of the time.

Music Stands

Not much needs to be said about music stands except to buy one. Again, you do not need a fancy or expensive stand. A simple fold-up wire stand will do. Too often, students place their music on a chair or a desk and crane their neck around to read the music. If you do this, you'll run the risk of developing bad posture and technique. Buy yourself a stand and be comfortable while you practice.

Sticks, Brushes, and Mallets

Sticks are the main implements you will use, and there are many varieties and models available. The companies with the best quality control are clearly Vic Firth and Regal Tip, but Promark, Zildjian, and Vater also make reputable sticks. For beginners, it is important to use a medium-sized stick such as the Vic Firth American Classic or the Regal Tip 5A. Do not use extremely skinny and short sticks, or conversely, very fat, heavy sticks, as they are designed for either very soft or very loud playing. As a beginner, you need a stick that will be versatile. Finally, buy only hickory or oak sticks. Stay away from maple sticks, as they are soft and will dent easily.

The standard tip or bead on the end of a stick is wooden. However, nylon tips are popular with many of today's drummers. Unfortunately, some rudimental drummers still reject nylon-tipped sticks, but, thankfully, this obstinate notion is dying away. The only real difference between wooden and nylon tips is that the latter has a brighter, more distinct tone on cymbals. For this reason, nylon tips work well in loud musical settings. Also, nylon tips are more durable.

Before purchasing a pair of sticks, hold each stick loosely, tap them together, and listen to the sound. A good pair of sticks should be pitch-matched. When each stick has the same pitch, your playing will sound more consistent and even.

Regardless of the brand, model, or tip, make certain you purchase straight, evenly weighted sticks. Also, don't let anyone sell you metal or plastic sticks. Stick shafts are always wooden! Metal and plastic sticks are novelty items and will only interfere with your ability to develop proper technique. Further, discounted sticks (you may see them lying around in boxes) are almost always defective and should be avoided. Finally, you will see different colored sticks such as black, white, and red. These are artist signature sticks and should be avoided, because, again, they are designed for specific uses. As you develop, you will want to experiment with different stick types, but for now, keep your selection simple and conservative.

Beginners needn't worry about purchasing brushes right away but be prepared to buy them should a performance opportunity arise. Brushes are metallic or nylon bristles that attach to a metal, wooden, or rubber shaft. The bristles fan out from the shaft and are raked across the drumhead or cymbal to create a subtle "white noise" effect. Say *Shhhhhh* aloud. The sound of your voice is not unlike the sound of a brush being combed across a snare drumhead.

Before purchasing a pair of sticks, make sure you first roll each stick on a flat surface. If the stick wobbles, that means that the stick is warped. Don't buy it! Misshapen sticks have an inconsistent tone and will only interfere with your performance.

Like sticks, brushes come in various shapes and sizes and are manufactured by several different companies. It's difficult to say which type or brand is best for you although the Regal Tip 550W and 583R are both very good. If you do buy brushes, make sure to buy the retractable kind. Retractable means that the brushes can be drawn back into the shaft. Often, brush companies refer to these as *telescoping brushes*. Nonretractable brushes have a shorter lifespan, because the exposed bristles often become tangled and bent like used paintbrushes.

FIGURE 1-3
Mallets, sticks, and brushes

As you might have guessed, mallets also come in many shapes and sizes. A mallet is a stick with a soft, rounded felt head. As a drum set player, you will want to use tympani mallets on your drums. Vic Firth and Musser (Ludwig) both make quality mallets. Vic Firth's T1 General is very good, as is the Musser Payson Model Medium Mallet (L-306). The drum set player uses mallets only to roll on tom-toms and cymbals, so you don't need to buy expensive, imported, or handmade mallets. Just about any name-brand semisoft felt mallet will meet your needs. **FIGURE 1-3** shows examples of sticks, brushes, and mallets.

Putting Together Your Setup

The ergonomics of drumming can't be understated. Proper positioning of your pads, drums, and cymbals is crucial to your success, because it affects both your posture and your technique. If you have a poor setup:

- You will become easily winded.
- You will be unable to maintain a consistent sound.
- You will be unable to maneuver properly around your kit.

- Your timing will suffer.
- You could injure your back, arms, wrists, and hands.

Proper Positioning of the Snare Drum or Pad

Many of the great teachers will tell you that the snare drum or pad should be positioned at your navel or belly button. For smaller children, since their bodies are not yet evenly proportioned, some adjustments may need to be made. Your arms should be in an L-shape formation at 90 degrees and the sticks should lay comfortably on top of the drum or pad in an upside down V shape.

If your sticks rest on the rim, the drum or pad needs to be lowered. Oppositely, if you find that you are leaning into the drum too much, the drum should be raised. As we will discuss in greater detail in Chapter 2, the sound you make is only the *end* result of your stroke, so in order to ensure efficiency of movement, you must make sure that the snare drum or pad is conveniently placed in front of you. This applies to both a sitting and standing position.

Those who use the traditional grip (see Chapter 2) often tilt their snare drum or pad so that the left side is slightly higher than the right. This is done to accommodate the turning motion in the left hand.

A Full Set

Setting up a full drum set (or pad set) properly is very important. First, set your drum throne so that your legs are at a 90-degree angle. In other words, when you place your feet on the pedals (hi-hat on left, bass drum on right) your legs should not be outstretched in an obtuse angle. Next, position your snare drum as previously described. Your 12" rack tom-tom should be placed about 1½" above the snare drum and tilted slightly toward you. If you have a 13" rack tom-tom, it should be evenly placed to the right of the 12" drum and also tilted toward you: a kind of mirror image of the 12" tom. The floor tom should be about 2" lower than your snare drum and can be tilted slightly in your direction. As you glide your arms in a clockwise motion around your kit, everything should feel accessible to you.

Place your ride cymbal to your right and position it so that your right arm is extended about 150 to 160 degrees. The stick should easily touch the main body of the cymbal (usually where the company logo is painted and the cymbal tapers or curves downward). If the stick is touching the bell or cup of the cymbal, the cymbal needs to be pulled further away from you. You will also want to tilt the cymbal toward you.

ALERT!

If you don't put a rug under your drum set, you will slide around, and your playing will suffer. Make sure, however you set up your drums, that everything stays where you put it!

The crash cymbal should be placed to your left but must be accessible to both hands. Like the ride, it, too, should be tilted but placed slightly higher than the ride cymbal so that you can strike the cymbal on the edge with the shaft of your stick.

Be advised that the setup shown in **FIGURE 1-4** is a basic drum setup. Certainly, you will see drummers experimenting with a wide variety of setups. However, before you go tinkering with different setups, get comfortable with the setup indicated here. Also, for all you lefties out there, simply follow these guidelines in reverse or, as many left-handed drummers do, get used to the standard right-handed setup. There are advantages to setting up right-handed even if you're a left-handed person. Finally, since pad sets are designed to simulate the look and feel of real drums, everything stated here applies to that setup as well.

Think about Your Commitment

Before you begin playing the drums, you'll need to think about what you want to get out of the experience. To be successful in your endeavors,

FIGURE 1-4
Drum setup

you will need to make drumming part of your everyday life and learn how to best structure your practice time. You will also need to keep your mind open to new ways of thinking altogether. You'll be surprised to learn that music has a mind, character, and will all its own. It's up to you to tap into the living consciousness that is music and drumming.

In addition, you will need to make smart purchases that help you to meet your musical goals but do not break the bank. Think long term. If you sense that you're in it for the long haul, buy equipment that will last through the beginning and intermediate phases of your development. One of your goals may be to form a band or join an already existing one. If you work hard, within a year's time, you'll possess enough skill to play with other musicians. Choose equipment now that will serve your intentions well and allow for maximum musical expression. Ⓔ

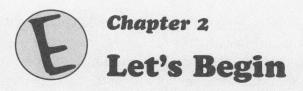

Chapter 2

Let's Begin

Before you even hit a drum, you'll need to consider how you sit or stand. The way you hold your sticks is also extremely important. Often, it's what you don't do that matters the most. Review the checklist found later in the chapter for a list of grip do's and don'ts. After you learn to hold the sticks, the next big challenge will be to learn how to strike the drum properly.

Posture

Back problems usually occur in the lower lumbar region of the spine, since this is the area of the body that supports the upper torso and is responsible for so much range of motion. Vertebrae, spinal disks, and back muscles can become susceptible to injury if you have poor posture at the drum set.

The proper posture for playing the drums is easy. Maintaining it is difficult. If you're lazy about your drumming posture, you could pay the price later on. For example, Don Henley, drummer for the Eagles, suffered a great deal from postural stress throughout his career. Don't let this happen to you.

Bill Bruford, one of the most innovative drummers of his time, claims that playing the drums is a lot like dancing. He is right! Drumming and dancing both rely on an interrelationship between your hands and feet, and both require great coordination and balance. Perhaps this is why so many drummers and dancers keep a mirror directly in front of themselves in the practice room or rehearsal studio. You should too. Like a ballet dancer, you need to observe carefully every movement you make.

ALERT!

When lifting your drums, or anything for that matter, always lift with your legs. Lifting with your back can cause serious injury.

Make sure your back is relaxed but straight and that you do not lean to one side. When you play, roll your shoulders back, but never tense them or raise them unnaturally. Since all facets of drumming are interconnected, you will eliminate a lot of bad habits right off the bat through observing and correcting your posture. This posture applies to both a standing and seated position.

You may ask, "But when would I stand to play my drum set?" You don't. Snare drummers who play in a concert band, orchestra, or marching band stand to play. Still, it is a posture you should be familiar with, because you never know where drumming will take you.

Hand Techniques

Before you even think about playing the drum set, you must first develop your hand technique. Unfortunately, some methods of playing can hurt you over time. The great rock drummer, Max Weinberg, has had multiple hand surgeries due to improper technique. He is not alone in this.

It's not uncommon for drummers to decide, far into their careers, that they need to go back and change the way they play. Some alter their approach because of an injury. Others gradually realize that they are not getting the musical results they desire. Top pros such as Steve Smith, Dave Weckl, and Neil Peart all went back into the proverbial "woodshed" and started over.

The Importance of Good Technique

The purpose of this section isn't to scare you or turn you into a musical hypochondriac. Simply recognize that drumming, like any other physical activity, can lead to health problems if you play improperly. The same is true with typing or playing tennis. Like drumming, these seemingly innocuous activities can cause strain or injury in the hands and arms.

The way you hold your sticks is probably the single most important facet in drumming. Stick control is influenced first and foremost by the grip you use. Success depends on your ability to use your wrists, forearms, and fingers well. Also, you will need to learn how to use fulcrums. All of this will be defined later in the chapter.

Don't Take Shortcuts

Like athletics, drumming is an aerobic exercise that requires efficiency of movement and the development of both your gross and fine motor skills. If you're serious about music and drumming, don't take the easy way out. Don't skip the following pages so that you can get on to the "fun stuff." You must have long-term vision and remain patient. Stay the course, and as you begin practicing, continually check for errors or deviations in your technique. Remember this: Once you get used to playing a certain way, whether right or wrong, it's very difficult to make a change. So be proactive and take charge now! You'll thank yourself down the road.

Grips and Fulcrums

There are two basic ways to grip the sticks: traditional and matched. The traditional grip comes from the military tradition and, as you might guess, is the oldest style of playing. The popular, even romanticized, image of the drummer boy should come to mind: the patriotic youngster marching off to war with his field drum strapped around his shoulder.

The Traditional Grip

The traditional grip was born of necessity. In order to play the drum with the left hand, the marching drummer naturally placed his stick in the web space of his hand, in between his thumb and forefinger, or pointer finger. The marching drummer would then swivel his forearm and wrist to strike the drum. This motion is similar to turning a doorknob.

To position his right hand, the marching drummer would turn his wrist so that his palm was flat. In clinical terms, this is called a pronated hand position. The drummer would then grasp the stick between his thumb and forefinger and use an up-and-down wrist motion. (See **FIGURE 2-1**.)

FIGURE 2-1
Traditional grip

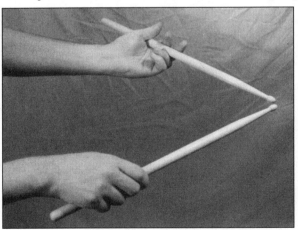

The traditional grip offers great subtlety of motion and promotes nuance and finesse in your playing. Jazz drummers, in particular, enjoy this grip because they are required to play a great deal of intricate rhythms with a soft touch. Also, some observe that the traditional grip encourages the drummer to create more flowing musical phrases. This is debatable though, since some of the most fluid drummers of today use the matched grip exclusively. The drummer for the Dave Matthews Band, Carter Beauford, is a good example of this. Some believe that the traditional grip is also better designed for playing the brushes. You will learn more about this in Chapter 17.

On the downside, the traditional grip lacks the power of the matched grip. By using a circular, whipping motion, you can play loudly with the traditional grip. However, the matched grip is less complicated. It's easier to cup the stick in the palm of your hand and use your wrist to strike the drum. If you want a lot of power, you simply add the forearm. When you play this way, the weight of your wrist and forearm allows you to hit the drum loudly and with little effort. The matched grip is also a very steady grip for soft dynamics.

FACT

The drummer for the Beatles, Ringo Starr, was one of the first to popularize the matched grip. His influence on pop culture contributed to the decline in traditional grip drummers.

In a perfect world, you should learn both matched and traditional grips because both grips offer subtle differences in sound and style. However, to tackle both grips all at once is foolish. Choose one grip and focus your energy on that. For the purposes of this book, we will concentrate on matched grip since it is the most popular way to hold the sticks. Matched grip is also the wave of the future.

That said, grip choice is ultimately your decision. Many drummers enjoy using the traditional grip for a whole assortment of reasons. If you do choose the traditional grip, keep in mind that what is detailed on the following pages will still apply to your right hand.

The Matched Grip

A fulcrum is a point against which something turns or is supported. For example, a hinge on a door is a fulcrum. Think of the fulcrum as a balance or pivot point. Using a matched grip, you will create a fulcrum by placing the stick between your thumb and forefinger and grasping or pinch-ing the stick. (See **FIGURE 2-2**.)

FIGURE 2-2
Matched grip

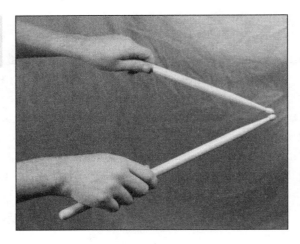

FIGURE 2-2
Matched grip

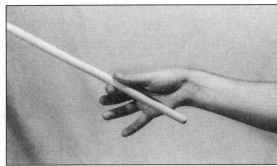

FIGURE 2-3
Lateral grasp

In academic parlance, this is called a lateral grasp. When you put a key into a lock, you hold the key between your thumb and forefinger using a lateral grasp. You will hold the drumstick with the same type of grasp. (See **FIGURE 2-3**.)

There are two balance points drummers use and both require a lateral grasp. Let's call these balance points fulcrum A and fulcrum B. Later in the book, you will learn the applications for these fulcrums. With fulcrum A, the stick should touch the pad of the thumb and the joint closest to your fingertip. The stick should not touch the underside or upper side of your finger. Instead, it should touch *only* the lateral side of your finger in between the under and upper sides.

Let's use a silly example to help you to understand this. Have you ever put your hand in the shape of a pistol? When you do this, your thumb is pointed upward and your forefinger is pointed outward; your forefinger acts as a make-believe pistol barrel. The top of the barrel is the area that would touch the drumstick.

Fulcrum B is very similar to Fulcrum A. The only difference is the joint placement on the forefinger. For fulcrum B, place the stick in between the pad of the thumb and the joint in the middle of your finger. Be careful. Never let the stick fall back against the joint closest to the palm of your hand or you will lose control.

Don't Squeeze

Always remember that you do not need to pinch the stick tightly. Grasp the stick loosely and avoid muscular tension. As you learn more about rudiments (Chapters 6 and 7) and drum set beats (Chapters 11, 12 and 13), you will further explore the uses of these two fulcrums.

You should grip the stick about ⅜ of the way up the shaft. This is a little below the halfway point. As you hold the stick, you should see what is commonly referred to as the "butt" of the stick. This is the end of the shaft opposite the tip. If you do not see the butt, you will need to choke up more. Try to gauge the equilibrium of the stick. Does the stick want to fall tip first or away from you or does the stick want to fall butt first or toward you? If you're holding the stick properly, it should fall tip first and away from you.

ALERT!

It's very important that you do not pinch the stick tightly or you will notice increased fatigue. Over time, a tight lateral grasp could strain the web muscles in your hands or cause tendonitis. It could even contribute to carpal tunnel syndrome.

After you've developed a proper lateral grasp, and positioned your fingers in the correct spot on the stick, all that's left to do is curve your index, ring, and pinkie fingers around the stick gently. Again, do not squeeze the stick. Keep these fingers relaxed, and, remember, you must hold the stick with your thumb and forefinger only. The index or middle finger may gently assist in balancing the stick, but it should not be treated as a legitimate member of the fulcrum family since it has a more important function. As you increase velocity, you will need the index finger to propel the stick. We will get into finger technique later.

Final Do's and Don'ts

Following is a list of grip do's and don'ts.

Do:
- Use the grips and fulcrums described earlier in the chapter.
- Keep your arms, wrists, and hands relaxed and in a natural position. If you feel stiff, loosen up.
- Hold the stick so that it feels slightly weighted toward the tip.

Don't:
- Hold the sticks like a club.
- Tense or lock your arms, wrists, or fingers.
- Extend your ring finger or pinkie finger outward. Keep them gently wrapped around the stick.
- Clench the stick. If someone were to accidentally knock your hands, your sticks should fall to the ground.

Creating a Sound

When striking a drum, you undergo the process of mental calculation and physical action all in a split second. Seasoned drummers know how to do this without much conscious effort; it just happens naturally. You can tell you're listening to a great drummer when you hear a variety of refined tones coming from the drums and cymbals. Check out the jazz drummers Shelly Manne, Ed Thigpen, and Peter Erskine or the rock/pop drummer Manu Katché. These players are very melodic in their approach. They, and others like them, all know how to create beautiful tones on their drums and cymbals.

How do you do this? The only way to learn how to create pleasing sounds is through trial and error and through observing and listening to professional drummers. As you progress, you will find that you naturally learn how to strike the drum with greater confidence, fluidity, and grace.

Before you even try to get a good sound, consider the elements that influence it. When you strike the drum or pad you should use one of the following.

1. Wrists
2. Forearms
3. Fingers
4. Combinations of the wrists, forearms, and fingers

These represent the four distinct but generalized techniques that drummers use. The next question is "How do I know which technique to use?" For every musical moment, you will need to make technical decisions based on dynamic or volume concerns and velocity or speed concerns.

It's important to note that both volume and speed are relative terms. What's fast to you may be slow to someone else or vice versa. What's loud to you may be soft to someone else or vice versa. Concern yourself only with what volume and speed mean to you given the technical abilities you currently possess.

When working through this book, start thinking about what part of your arms—wrists, forearms, fingers, or a combination of the three—works best for what you are playing. Don't expect to know these answers right away. This kind of insight takes a long time. Start by exploring how each technique is affected by volume and speed. Gradually you'll discover what works best.

Wrist Movement

The wrist can accommodate both very soft and medium-loud playing. Also, the wrist can withstand fairly quick tempi, or speed. Because the wrist's dynamic range is quite large, and its tempo range is also quite broad, you will end up using your wrist more than any other part of your arm; the wrist is especially great for dynamic levels and tempi that are in your "comfortable zone."

Like the drummer boy's right-hand technique, turn your wrists so that your palm is almost completely flat. Next, move your wrist up and down. This is the only wrist motion that is acceptable. Often, students play from their elbow and keep their thumbs pointed upward. This is incorrect unless you are riding on a cymbal. Observe your wrists as you play. Are your wrists moving up and down? They should be. Are your forearms moving up and down? They should *not* be. For now, limit any and all movement to your wrists.

The Forearm

The forearm can be used to play slow, soft musical passages. The weight of the arm can help you to play more steadily and consistently. However, the forearm is not generally used to play fast. Your wrist and fingers can achieve fast speeds much more easily and with much less tension. Quite often, the forearm is used for extremely high volumes and accentuation in music. The forearm also does not work well in conjunction with the fingers.

Using Your Fingers

The index, ring, and pinkie fingers are separate from the fulcrum. They cannot produce a loud sound and are used mostly to play fast flurries of notes or motorlike passages in music. Your fingers also never work directly in combination with the forearm to produce a single note. You may have whipping arm accents followed by subtle finger manipulations but this would never occur on the same note.

You have to start somewhere. For now, don't stifle your playing by being overly concerned about finger and forearm use. Focus on wrist development. Most students find that over time they naturally develop a sense for finger and arm movement. However, if you fail to first develop the proper wrist technique, everything that comes after will suffer.

The fingers do often work in conjunction with the wrist. The wrist and forearm also work together a lot. This will become clear to you as you learn to play the long roll or double stroke roll and the other rudiments listed in Chapters 6 and 7.

Where to Hit the Drum or Pad

Grasp the stick using the fulcrum A, then turn your wrist in a palm-flat position. Next, hover the sticks about ⅛" above the drum in an upside-down V formation. The tips of the sticks should almost touch.

Find the center of the drum or pad and position the sticks about ¾" above the center, as shown in **FIGURE 2-4**.

This is the ideal place to strike the drum when playing at a medium to loud dynamic. As you get softer, you will need to move toward the rim of the drum to maintain a good sound. For most of the playing required in this book, target your playing to the area about ¾" above or north of the center.

FACT

The batter head on your snare drum (or some types of pads) will eventually wear down and you will see how accurate your playing really is. If your playing is spot-on, this worn patch shouldn't be much larger than a quarter.

Listening for Consistency

When you practice, make sure that you remain mentally focused and engage in meaningful instruction with yourself. In order to be successful, you must be both the student and the teacher. In other words, you must assess and critique your own playing every step of the way. The only way to do this is through listening. Following is a list of questions you should ask yourself when practicing the exercises in this book:

• Am I playing the rhythms evenly?
• Is my tempo steady, dragging, or rushing?

- Is one hand louder than the other hand?
- Am I playing in the proper area of the head or is one hand straying? You should be able to tell this by listening as well as seeing.
- Do I sound stiff or relaxed?

ALERT!

If you feel pain or fatigue when you practice, stop. Take a break! Drumming is not bodybuilding. The phrase "no pain, no gain" does not apply here.

A Word to the Wise

Some musicians believe that the less they know, the more unique their playing will be. This is not entirely baseless. Beginners possess a naiveté that can yield interesting musical results. Untrained musicians have also been known to play music that sounds fresh and uninhibited. However, the "less is more" philosophy is commonly misunderstood by students. This idea refers to artistic concerns, not to the technique that informs it.

Your prime directive should be to attain skill and knowledge. Enter into the mainstream and root yourself into the musical culture. Later, if you choose, you can be a nonconformist. For now, don't worry about being original or innovative. You must first learn to communicate well musically. Spending a lot of your time developing "chops," as musicians call it, is always time well spent. Musical technique is not unlike serving a tennis ball, pitching a slider, or teeing off on the golf course. All of these activities require specific movements and physical disciplines. Don't make up your own techniques.

Holding the sticks with the correct fulcrums, using the proper wrist motion, and maintaining good posture are essential baby steps in your musical growth. Don't interfere in this process by misinterpreting the "less is more" approach to music. More is more. Learn everything you can about technique and you will be able to contribute better to the great collective musical conversation. When you display proper form and technique, you have more musical options, and your creativity will soar.

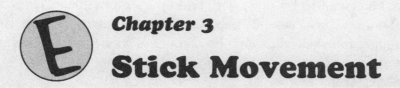

Chapter 3

Stick Movement

Now that you are holding the sticks properly and have placed your focus on wrist movement, it's time to learn about the three most important strokes you will use: the full stroke, the half stroke, and the tap stroke. At the end of this chapter, you'll also learn how to use your fingers and arms.

Strokes

When a drummer refers to stick movement, he or she is talking about strokes. Any time you strike the drum, you use a stroke. As you may have guessed, proficiency with strokes leads toward technical mastery in general. The three strokes focused on here (the full stroke, half stroke, and taps) all consist of a downward and upward movement. They also all use bounce. The difference between these strokes lies only in the placement of the sticks' tips and the amount of wrist snap you use.

Control Strokes

There are three additional strokes that you should know about. These strokes are called down strokes, upstrokes, and dead strokes. The down stroke begins with the tip of the stick pointed straight in the air like a minute hand on twelve o'clock. After you strike the drum, you do not let the sticks rebound back to twelve o'clock. Instead, you restrict the sticks so that they hover about ½" above the drumhead. By doing this, only a downward motion has been achieved.

The upstroke begins where the down stroke leaves off. The sticks are placed about ½" above the drumhead. You then snap your wrists and strike the drum. The important feature is the upward motion that follows. After you hit the drum, your wrists fling the sticks into a twelve o'clock position. By doing this, an upward motion is achieved.

The dead stroke is exactly the same as the down stroke except that you press the stick into the drumhead. You do not raise the stick off the head after each stroke. Instead, you let the stick sink into the drum, choking the head so that it does not vibrate.

These three strokes are included in this book mostly as an advisory. If you take lessons someday, these strokes will undoubtedly be discussed, and it's best to be given a quick overview of them. Don't confuse the down, up, and dead stroke with the full and half strokes or taps. They are very different.

The Primary Strokes

Full, half, and tap strokes allow for tension-free playing. They also rely on bounce or rebound. Down, up, and dead strokes tend to promote stiff playing, wasted motion, and a poor sound. They are not all bad, but they should be used only with care. As a beginner, it's important to know about them if only to avoid them for the time being.

For example, the dead stroke is often confused with the full stroke. The dead stroke is a novelty stroke. Its uses are extremely limited and therefore you shouldn't monkey with it. As they say, leave it to the professionals. You do not want to press the stick into the drum when you play.

When learning the full, half, and tap strokes, economy of motion is the name of the game. Dexterity and fluidity depend almost entirely on your ability to play with the least amount of physical activity. Expend the *least* amount of physical effort when drumming. This doesn't mean that you play with lazy technique or appear lethargic on the bandstand. Drumming is all about harnessing your energy and, through bounce, harnessing the sticks' potential.

The Importance of Bounce

Rebound or bounce is the catalyst for speed and relaxed playing. It also allows you to get a great full sound with very little effort. If you're holding the sticks loosely, the tips of the sticks will rebound back toward you after you strike the drum. This is related in Newton's Third Law. This fundamental law of physics states that "for every action there is an equal and opposite reaction."

As you learn the strokes described in the following, you must allow the sticks to bounce. If you grasp them too tightly, this bounce will not occur. With each stroke, there is a shift in the trajectory of the stick from the start point to the end point then back up to the starting point again. Tension in your hands, wrists, or arms will interfere with this movement and cut off the bounce. Grasping the stick with your index, ring, and pinkie fingers will also choke each stroke and not allow for bounce.

You do not want to bring the sticks back to the original start point by forcing them. Don't cheat! Never manually bring the sticks back to the start position by flexing your wrists back upward. If you're playing properly, the sticks should automatically return to the start point all by themselves through the use of the bounce.

The sticks may want to bounce multiple times. On the rebound, they may also want to overshoot the initial start point. Don't worry. All you will need to do is gently squeeze your fingers together. This will stop, or arrest, the stick after each stroke. You will only need to do this at slow tempi. During a drum roll, for example, you will not have this problem because the sticks will remain in constant motion.

ALERT!

Once you use your fingers to stop the sticks' movement, you must again resume a completely relaxed, noninterfering finger position in order to play the next note. Also, any finger gestures you use should be subtle. Don't strangle the stick.

Diligence in Practice

Developing quality strokes will be difficult and even a little boring to practice. This is where patience and a strong work ethic must come in. Try not to get frustrated or antsy. Calmly spend whatever time is necessary to address this issue. It will be well worth your while in the long run.

Some techniques teach you to play strenuously. They teach you to huff and puff and sweat profusely when you're on the stage. The method outlined here is derived from the greatest technicians drumming has ever produced. If you embrace the techniques discussed here, you will learn to play with control and greater dynamic range. You will also learn how to play with a great sound.

The concept of "less is more" applies well to this situation. The key to developing great technique is to never force anything. You may get temporary results by "muscling" the stick, but in the end, you will find that this only causes fatigue and stiffness.

It's very easy to move too much when drumming. If you're running out of breath or if your arms are getting tired, chances are you're using what fusion-jazz drummer Dave Weckl calls "the athletic approach" to drumming. You will want to avoid this approach, as he does, by holding the sticks loosely and playing tension-free. Some players flail their arms around when they perform. They add a lot of theatrics to their drumming. This is all show. As the legendary jazz drummer Joe Morello once said, "It looks good, but it doesn't show up on records."

Strike a hard table or countertop two different ways. First, squeeze the stick as tightly as possible and strike. This sound will be choked and thin. Second, hold the stick very loosely and strike the table. You will notice that the second sound is fuller and warmer. You will also hear the tone of the stick as it vibrates. Listen for this when you play on real drums.

Action and Reflex Reaction

All strokes require a reflex reaction. You must first put the sticks into action by snapping your wrist down. You must then control the sticks' movement through a reaction. This reaction must be instantaneous. The only way to do this is through your reflexes. The first time you get the sticks to bounce, they will seem a lot like Mexican jumping beans. Gaining proficiency with strokes means gaining control of the bounce. In the heat of the moment, there is no time to think.

A reflex is not something you learn. It's hard-wired into you and is a function of the spinal cord. If you accidentally touch a hot oven, you pull away instantly. No one taught you how to do that. Controlling the bounce requires this same kind of reaction. You will need to apply what your body already knows to drumming. Along the way, keep your wrists loose and allow your hands to follow the natural trajectory of the sticks. If you do this, you will realize that you can play faster and with greater ease. You will also be able to concentrate on the music and not your hands.

The Full Stroke

When you play strokes you must use specific start and end points. The full stroke represents the highest start point. To play this, you must first turn your wrists in a palm-flat position. Next, arch your wrists upward, snap them down one at a time, and let each stick rebound back to its original start point. The start position is where the tips of the sticks point directly upward. As with the down stroke, if the stick were a minute hand, the tip would be on twelve o'clock when it's in the start position.

ALERT!

When preparing for a full stroke, do not place the stick in a position that points backward; it must be exactly straight up. This stick will never go past the twelve o'clock position.

Practice full strokes every day until they become easy and natural. Use an alternating method. Play slow, steady strokes beginning with the left hand, then the right hand, and so on. You may also start with the right hand and move right to left in an alternating fashion. It's important that you always alternate so that each hand gets the same workout.

If you are having trouble getting a bounce, temporarily pinch the stick in between your forefinger and index finger. Snap the stick down with your wrist in a palm-flat position. The tip of the stick should bounce back toward you as the butt end is thrust away from you. By doing this, you will feel the bounce easier. Just remember, this is not normally how you will hold the sticks.

You can also try bouncing a tennis ball or superball on your drum. Snap the ball, then catch it on the rebound. The sticks should bounce just as freely as the ball. When you snap the sticks down, you are actually releasing them. You then catch the sticks as they return to the start position. Try this catch, release, catch, release movement with each hand until you develop the mechanical skill to do it effortlessly. If you drop the sticks a few times along the way, don't worry. Just make sure that when you snap the sticks down, your hand always remains in contact with the sticks.

Unlike the ball analogy, you must keep your index, ring, and pinkie fingers curved around the sticks at all times. This does not mean that you are grabbing the sticks with your fingers. You are simply maintaining your hand placement. You must also keep your fulcrum intact when you perform this release-catch stroke. If you do not do this, you will lose control of the bounce and your ability to play accurately will be greatly diminished.

Observe videos of Buddy Rich or Joe Morello. When they play, the sticks seem to come alive, or jump, on their drums and cymbals. It's no illusion; the sticks are actually doing this. This occurs as the nonflexible stick comes into contact with the taut drumhead. In simple terms this is called a bounce. These two are moving so fast that their reflexes are almost in full command of their stick movement.

The Half Stroke

The half stroke is similar to the full stroke. In fact, everything that applies to the full stroke applies equally to the half stroke. The only difference is the starting point. Rather than starting at twelve o'clock, place the sticks at three o'clock or slightly higher. Again, snap the sticks down with your wrists and allow them to bounce back to their original position. You will use the release-catch method as before and you must practice this stroke by alternating your hands in a slow, steady fashion.

You will find that the half stroke is more difficult to play because you have less snapping power to create a bounce. You will have less power because you are starting at a lower point. The result is a softer sound. This is desirable. Half strokes will not be used for playing accents or loud notes. They will be used only to play faster medium-loud notes or slower medium-loud notes. You also will notice that the half stroke is quite manageable and useful. In fact, you will use the half stroke more than any other stroke.

Taps

Taps are very soft. They are used to play grace notes, ghost notes, and piano to pianissimo (soft to very soft) dynamics. Later, when you learn the flam (Chapter 7), you will experiment with taps. As with the full and half strokes, taps consist of a down-up and release-catch motion. Also like full and half strokes, you will want to play taps at a slow, steady speed. Always alternate your hands when practicing them.

In order to create a tap, place the sticks about 1" or so above the drumhead or pad. Do not snap the stick down. Instead, drop the stick onto the head and catch it on the rebound. For a grace note, you will tap the drum just prior to a louder, main note. This kind of tap is played only a fraction of a second before the main note. Say *fa-lam* aloud and you will hear the effect of a grace note through onomatopoeia. The *f* equals the grace note and the *lam* equals the main note.

Ghost notes represent another use for the tap. Smooth musical gestures can be created by using this type of tap. Ghost notes are not heard distinctly. They may not even be detected by the listener. Ghost notes beef up or round out the sound of rhythms. They add a kind of echo or hum to the rhythms being played. In reality, ghost notes make rhythms sound less angular by infusing them with dynamic depth. This all makes the music come alive with vibrant textures. You will put taps to use when you learn about beats and fills.

How to Use Your Arms and Fingers

In Chapter 2, you learned when to use your arms and fingers but you didn't learn how to use them. Before you begin to think about using these parts of your body, make sure that you're proficient with your wrists. As a beginner, you will still need to focus most of your energy on wrist competency. The arm should be least important to you. Once you learn to use the wrist and fingers both separately and in combination, you can start working on arm movement.

Arm Techniques

There are several arm techniques and all of them have subtle name variations. When drumming, you'll only need to use the arms to maneuver around the drum set and to create very loud accents. There are two arm movements you should know about. They are the whip throw and the straight forearm throw. Be careful with the latter, because it promotes stiffer playing.

Whipping action requires that your arms remain entirely relaxed. Lift your arms from the shoulder and let your elbows extend outward. Snap your arms down, one at a time, striking the drum with a whiplike motion. Allow your arms and wrists to bend as you do this; you do not want to slam the stick into the drum with your arms locked up. In the start position, the wrist will hang downward. When you move, the elbow whips in toward your ribs and the wrist naturally straightens out as you whap the drum. Make sure the wrist stays in the palm-flat position as you do this.

Whipping action is used for very loud accents. However, it cannot be used for multiple accents in a row. This is where the straight forearm throw comes in. This is the only technique that requires that you lock your wrists in a palm-flat position. When you do this, you are forced to play entirely from the elbow. In other words, your forearm is the catalyst for sound. Karl Perazzo, the timbale player with Carlos Santana, performs the straight forearm throw impeccably.

FACT

As a drum set player, the straight forearm throw should be used sparingly. It is only used when you absolutely must play a series of very loud accents. Even if you're playing rock stadiums, you should not have to use this technique often. The whipping arm motion—in combination with your wrists and fingers—should cover just about everything you'll need to play, even in loud settings.

Using Your Fingers

Fingers take on an extremely important role since they often work in combination with the wrists. You will learn about such combinations when you study the rudiments. Fingers have a way of monopolizing the single stroke roll, for example, and they also allow you to attain very fast speeds on all other rolls and paradiddles. For now, you only need to learn about basic finger movements. You'll apply these movements to drumming in Chapter 6.

When you grasp the stick using either fulcrum A or B, your other three fingers (index, ring, and pinkie) are not active. However, they do have a role in drumming. These fingers can be used to propel the stick. If you press these fingers against the palm of your hand, the sticks will move away from you. When you release these fingers, the sticks will return to their start points. If you move your fingers in a steady, pulsating rhythm, you will see the sticks move back and forth quite naturally. If you're only using fingers—in other words, no wrists—you will need to turn your forearm so that your thumbs are pointed upward. This position is the opposite of palm flat. If you are playing in combination with your wrists, you will place your hands in a position that is halfway between the palm-flat and thumbs-up positions. In other words, your hand will be at an angle.

Letting It Flow Naturally

In performance situations, you should not consciously think about the strokes or movements you make. You should play freely, letting your hands and arms move naturally and comfortably. However, you will not be able to play this way unless you first spend a good portion of your practice time training your hands and arms to do this on their own.

Don't be afraid to be honest with yourself regarding your success rate. Critique first and devise strategies for improvement, but don't forget to take a moment to reflect on the positive aspects of your playing as well.

When you're learning to drum without the help of a teacher, it's difficult to gauge your success with strokes and other movements. Use a mirror to examine your movements. Also, record yourself when practicing. Compare recordings weekly and monitor your improvement or lack thereof. If each week you notice that you can play a little faster, a little more evenly, and with greater dynamic range, you are making progress. Ⓔ

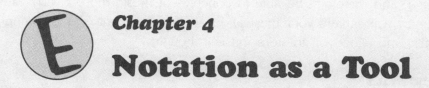

Chapter 4

Notation as a Tool

Musicians use notation to study music and to communicate musical ideas. In this chapter, you will learn the "nuts and bolts" of musical notation. Included in this tutorial will be information on notes, rests, time signatures, measures, bar lines, and much more. You will find that having the ability to read music makes life as a musician a lot easier and a lot more rewarding.

Notation Overview

Why should you learn how to read music? You should learn how to read music for the same reasons you learn how to read words. If you're musically literate, your chances of survival in the world of music greatly improve. By learning to read music you will be able to visualize music better, and therefore, be able to conceive of music more clearly. Musical literacy will expand your musical vocabulary, augment your communication skills, and allow you to store musical thoughts.

The Benefits

By becoming musically literate you will learn at a much faster pace. You will get "inside" of music a lot easier. You will see the possibilities of rhythm and delve deeper into both the mechanics and the art of music making. Like words, notation is a tool used to express and preserve musical ideas. Needless to say, its impact on musical history is colossal.

Notes, Rests, and the Staff

All music can be divided into two parts: sound and silence. Notes represent the sounds a musician makes. Rests indicate silence. Both are

FIGURE 4-1
A blank staff

written on a staff. A staff is a set of five parallel lines on which a composer writes notes, rests, and other musical symbols. (See **FIGURE 4-1**.)

The lines and spaces on a staff represent pitch varieties and a clef is used to name each line and space. The most common clefs are treble or G clef and bass or F clef, though alto and tenor clefs also exist. The

FIGURE 4-2
Neutral clef
with label

neutral clef suits drums the best, because its lines and spaces have no specific pitch qualities. (See **FIGURE 4-2**.)

Your drums are not pitch specific, so staves may or may not be used for snare drum music. A drum set, on the other hand, does require a staff since the lines and spaces will represent different drums and cymbals. There is little uniformity between publishers when it comes to drum set music. Therefore, most composers and copyists will use a key or legend to tell you what each line and space represents. Some rules still apply though.

Lower-pitched instruments such as the bass drum and floor tom-tom are always placed on the bottom half of the staff, while higher-pitched instruments such as the hi-hat or ride cymbal are placed on the top half of the staff. The snare drum is usually placed on the third space from the bottom, just above the middle line.

Notes and Rests

A note is made up of a note head and a note stem. A note head is seen either as an empty circle (whole or half notes) or as a colored-in dot (all other notes). A note stem is a vertical line that is attached to the note head. Sometimes notes are connected or barred together by a single horizontal line. This is used to indicate eighth notes. Sometimes you will see a double horizontal line. This is used to indicate sixteenth notes. Some notes have a wavy line that curves down the stem. This is called a flag. A single flag is used to signify eighth notes. A double flag is used to signify sixteenth notes. The different types of notes can be seen in **FIGURE 4-3**.

whole   half   quarter   eighth   barred eighths   sixteenth   barred sixteenths

FIGURE 4-3   A whole note, a half note, a quarter note, a single eighth note, two eighth notes barred together, a single sixteenth note, and two sixteenth notes barred together

Observe that an individual eighth note looks exactly the same as a quarter note but with a flag attached to it. The individual sixteenth note also looks like the quarter note but with two flags attached to it.

The British use different names for notes. They call a whole note a *semibreve*, a half note a *minim*, a quarter note a *crochet*, an eighth note a *quaver*, and a sixteenth note a *semiquaver*. Don't be confused by this and, unless you're in the UK, don't use these terms.

Table of Notes

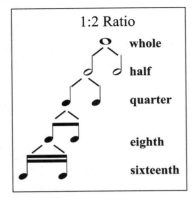

1:2 Ratio

whole
half
quarter
eighth
sixteenth

Musical notation is based on mathematics. Notation follows the same rules as fractions. **FIGURE 4-4** shows the division of notes.

As you can see, notes divide into two equal parts. A whole note divides into two half notes, a half note divides into two quarter notes, a quarter note divides into two eighth notes, and an eighth note divides into two sixteenth notes. When making these divisions, a 1:2 ratio occurs between the whole and half note, the half and quarter note, the quarter and eighth note, and the eighth and sixteenth note. **FIGURES 4-5** through **4-8** should help to make this clearer.

FIGURE 4-5
Divisional foundation of notes—half notes

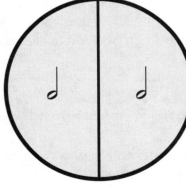

FIGURE 4-6
Divisional foundation of notes—quarter notes

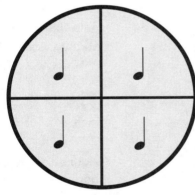

FIGURE 4-7
Divisional foundation of notes—eighth notes

FIGURE 4-8
Divisional foundation of notes—sixteenth notes

Observe that two half notes equals the whole pie, four quarter notes equals the whole pie, eight eighth notes equals the whole pie, and sixteen sixteenth notes equals the whole pie. This is the mathematical backbone of notation.

Rests

Rests function in exactly the same way as notes but with one key difference. Whereas a note signifies sound, a rest equals silence. A rest does not mean to pause. The music continues whether you're resting or not or whether there is sound or not. Think of a rest as a silent note.

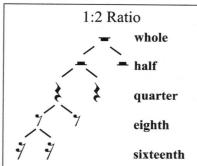

When resting, always follow the music the same as if you were playing. Every note has a corresponding rest and rests have the same relationship to one another as notes do. **FIGURE 4-9** shows each type of rest as it is divided from whole to sixteenth.

Piecing It Together

Now that you have been exposed to notes and rests, you must piece them together to make musical sentences. There are still other notational elements you must learn about in order to accomplish this.

Time Signatures

There are many time signatures used in music. In this chapter, we will focus only on 4/4 time. 4/4 is the most frequently used time signature, hence its nickname "common time."

All time signatures contain a top number and a bottom number. These numbers tell the musician two important things:

1. How many beats there are in a measure
2. What note value equals one beat

This definition requires an understanding of additional jargon, namely what a measure and a beat are. Music is played in time; it has a pulse that once started continues until the composition reaches its end. This pulse is the called the beat.

Notes and rests are segmented into smaller compartments of time. These boxes of time are called measures or bars. Notes and rests are contained within measures, and bar lines are used to demarcate each measure's borders. As you will see in **FIGURE 4-10**, bar lines are simple vertical lines used to separate measures.

FIGURE 4-10
Measure and bar lines

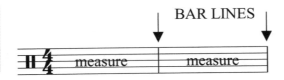

Let's return to time signatures. Think of 4/4 time as a fraction. Fractions have a top number called a numerator and a bottom number called a denominator. For our purposes, the numerator will tell you how many beats you have in a measure. The denominator will tell you what note value equals one beat. In order to do this though, you must first replace the numerator with a one.

Since there is a four in the numerator, we can say that there are four beats in each measure. If we temporarily take away the top four and place a one in the numerator, we are left with 1/4, or a quarter. This tells us that the quarter note equals the beat. So, 4/4 means we have four beats in a measure and the quarter note represents each beat.

The Repeat Sign

Before we practice reading music, you need to know about one other notational symbol. The repeat sign indicates one of two things. It either tells you to go back to the beginning of the music and play it one more time, or it tells you to return to its counterpart repeat sign and replay the portion of the music in between the two signs. In this chapter, all repeat signs tell you to go back to the beginning of the figure and play it one more time. **FIGURE 4-11** shows what the repeat signs look like.

FIGURE 4-11
Repeat signs

The Almighty Quarter Note

Quarter notes function as the pulse, or beat, in most of the music you will play. This is because 4/4 time is used almost exclusively in popular music. It is even used more than any other time signature in ethnic and jazz music. If you turn on the radio and flip through stations, 98 percent of the music you will hear uses the quarter note as its heartbeat. When we place four quarter notes into a measure of 4/4, we will count them as shown in **FIGURE 4-12**.

FIGURE 4-12
One bar of quarter notes

Each quarter note represents a downbeat. In 4/4, downbeats equal the numbers one, two, three, and four. When you practice, you should count all downbeats aloud.

If we divide quarter notes into eighth notes, we will have eight of them per measure, as shown in **FIGURE 4-13**.

FIGURE 4-13
One bar of eighth notes

We have now divided the beat into two parts and it should be counted "one-and, two-and, three-and, four-and." The *ands* represent upbeats in music. When they occur in the music you are playing, you should count them aloud, too.

Professionals do not count out loud when they are performing. However, counting out loud is crucial in the practice room, especially for beginners. Counting will help you to make sense of the rhythms you are reading.

No matter what, you must always count off before you begin drumming. This applies to both beginners and professionals. A tempo must always be established in order to play music. Music exists in time and space. Counting off solidifies the tempo and helps to avoid musical train wrecks.

Several exercises have been written out for you on the following pages. The idea is to expose you to common rhythms and to jump-start the process of learning to read music. Before each exercise you play, count off by saying aloud "one, two, three, four." Make sure you count off at a steady pace and be certain to actually play the tempo you count off. A common mistake is counting and playing at two different speeds.

If you feel that you've counted off too slowly or too fast, stop and start again. Never rush or drag in order to reach the desired tempo and always keep your counting and playing synchronized.

You should get in the habit of using a metronome when you practice. A metronome is a device that marks time with an electronic click. See Chapter 10 for information on using metronomes.

Basic Reading Exercises

By practicing the following exercises, you will cement your knowledge and, most importantly, put your skills to use. In Chapter 5, you will practice longer etudes but you must first begin with short four- and eight-bar phrases to help you to grasp the concepts presented in this chapter. The only way to learn how to read music is to actually do it.

Things to remember when practicing are:

- Be sure to play steady time; do not rush or drag.
- Count off before you play.
- Count out loud while you play.
- Follow the indicated sticking; R means right and L means left.
- Use only full, half, or tap strokes; concentrate more on the full and half stroke.
- Listen and play along with the accompanying CD, on which many of these exercises are performed for you.
- Record yourself playing and listen back. Be your own teacher. Are you rushing? Are you playing on rests? Are you forgetting repeats? Ask yourself questions and critique your performances.

The first exercise (**FIGURE 4-14**) is a series of alternating quarter notes. Make sure that your eyes follow every note on the page. It's tempting to memorize the pattern and look elsewhere as you play, but avoid this at all costs. If you don't follow the notes as they go by, you'll defeat the whole purpose of this exercise.

In **FIGURE 4-15**, you are asked to play a series of quarter notes. However, beats two and four have been turned into quarter rests. You will strike the drum only on beats one and three. Remember to count beats two and four as you play.

In the following exercise—**FIGURE 4-16**—you will strike the drum on beats two and four. The rests occur on beats one and three. This is the inverse of **FIGURE 4-15**.

 FIGURE 4-14   Eight bars of quarter notes

FIGURE 4-15   Quarter notes and quarter rests

FIGURE 4-17 combines the lessons learned in **FIGURES 4-14, 4-15,** and **4-16**. Be very careful with this exercise and do not move on to the next figure until you can play this one without any errors.

Before we combine quarter notes and eighth notes in music, you must first try practicing eighth notes alone, as in **FIGURE 4-18**. Eighth notes

FIGURE 4-16   Quarter rests and quarter notes

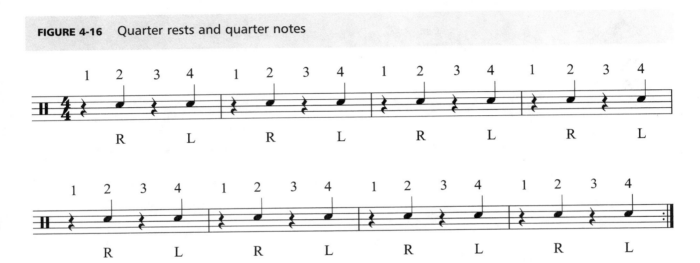

TRACK 2

FIGURE 4-17   Quarter note and quarter rest combination

will be played twice the speed of quarter notes. It is very important to feel the quarter note pulse when you practice eighth notes or any other notes for that matter. Remember, the quarter note is the pulse in 4/4.

Once you've mastered the preceding eighth note pattern, you can begin to combine eighth notes with quarter notes. **FIGURE 4-19** uses four two-bar

FIGURE 4-18 Eight bars of eighth notes

TRACK 3

FIGURE 4-19 Quarter note and eighth note combination

patterns followed by a repeat sign. Before you try playing all the way through the exercise, play each pattern first. You may even want to make an eight-bar exercise out of each two-bar pattern before you try playing the entire figure. Each pattern has been numbered so that you know where it begins.

FIGURE 4-20 brings back quarter rests. Again, you have been asked to play four two-bar patterns. They are numbered so that you know where each pattern begins. Play each pattern individually first. After you've mastered each pattern, put them together to create one eight-measure phrase with repeat.

Next, eighth rests have been added to the mix. The exercise in **FIGURE 4-21** is the same as **FIGURE 4-19** but with some of the downbeats extracted. All of the eighth rests written here occur on downbeats. Make sure you are counting out loud and remember that a rest is really a silent note. When you come to a rest, try to feel it internally. Try imagining a sound on the rest. This will help you to feel their presence.

In general, you will be able to play the exercises in this book more accurately if you devise some method for experiencing rests. Some

FIGURE 4-20   Quarter notes, quarter rests, and eighth notes

musicians make a physical movement of some kind. They nod their head or tap their toe inside their shoe. If you do this, make sure that these actions are not too dramatic. They should be very subtle. Tapping your foot loudly on the floor is a bad habit that should be avoided.

Sixteenth notes are played twice the speed of eighth notes or four times the speed of quarter notes. When playing the exercises in **FIGURE 4-22**, it's important not to lose track of the downbeat, or quarter-note pulse. Sixteenth notes will be counted "one-e-and-ah, two-e-and-ah, three-e-and-ah, four-e-and-ah." Don't worry about playing at a fast tempo. Just play them steady and count aloud.

Once you get comfortable with straight sixteenth notes, you will need to learn some of the common sixteenth note/quarter note combinations. In **FIGURE 4-23** you will find an eight-bar phrase that can further be broken up into two-bar patterns. Like **FIGURES 4-19** and **4-20**, each pattern will be numbered so that you know where each one begins. Also like **FIGURES 4-19** and **4-20**, you should practice the patterns individually, then put them together as one eight-bar phrase.

FIGURE 4-21 Quarter notes, eighth notes, and eighth rests

TRACK 4

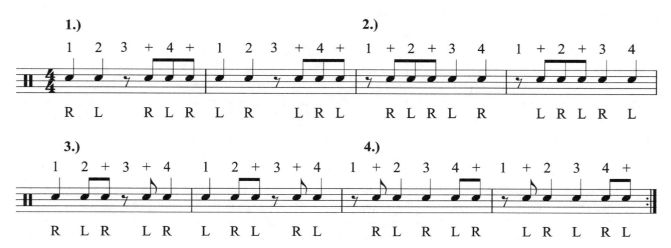

In the following two exercises, you will learn some of the common eighth note/sixteenth note combinations. The exercise in **FIGURE 4-24** contains one eighth note followed by two sixteenth notes. This rhythm is repeated four times per measure. It is counted "one-and-ah, two-and-ah, three-and-ah, four-and-ah."

FIGURE 4-22   Sixteenth notes

TRACK 5

FIGURE 4-23   Quarter notes and sixteenth notes

It is very easy to fall into triplets when playing this exercise. Triplets are three evenly spaced notes. This pattern is not supposed to be evenly spaced. Refer to the table of notes. The eighth note is worth two sixteenth notes; therefore, these notes will have an uneven feel to them. Make sure you cross-reference with the CD before you play this exercise.

The next pattern is the inverse of **FIGURE 4-24**. You are asked to play two sixteenth notes followed by one eighth note. When playing **FIGURE 4-25**, you will count "one-e-and, two-e-and, three-e-and, four-e-and." Again, make sure you do not fall into a triplet pattern. To avoid this common pitfall, refer to the table of notes and the CD and always count aloud.

The pattern in **FIGURE 4-26** uses combinations of **FIGURES 4-22, 4-24,** and **4-25** and is broken up into four two-bar phrases. Assuming that you have command of the rhythms found in the previous figures, you should be able to piece this exercise together without too much trouble. The hard part will be making the transition from one rhythmic type to the next. You may find that bridging the measures together is easier when you concentrate on two-bar phrases, then four-bar phrases, then six-bar phrases, and so on until you can move smoothly through the whole exercise with the repeat. Play at a slow tempo, count out loud, and make sure that you refer to the CD.

FIGURE 4-24 One eighth note and two sixteenth notes combination

FIGURE 4-25 Two sixteenth notes and one eighth note combination

TRACK 7

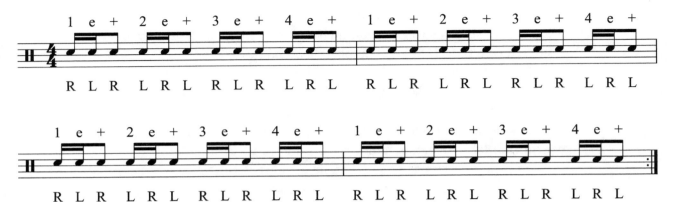

FIGURE 4-26 Sixteenth note/eighth note combinations

FIGURE 4-27 is identical to FIGURE 4-26 except that quarter and eighth notes have replaced some of the sixteenths or eighth/sixteenth combinations.

FIGURE 4-28 is identical to FIGURE 4-27 except that some downbeats and upbeats have been taken out and quarter and eighth rests have been added respectively.

FIGURE 4-27   Quarter, eighth, and sixteenth note combinations

TRACK 8

FIGURE 4-28   Adding quarter and eighth rests

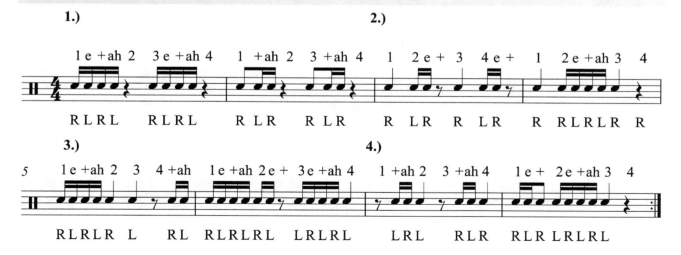

Use of sixteenth rests can be very difficult. The exercise in **FIGURE 4-29** is identical to **FIGURE 4-22** except for one significant change. Sixteenth rests have replaced all four downbeats in each measure.

The exercise in **FIGURE 4-30** is also based on **FIGURE 4-22**. The difference here is that you now have sixteenths rests on both the downbeats and the upbeats.

FIGURE 4-29 Sixteenth rests on downbeats

TRACK 9

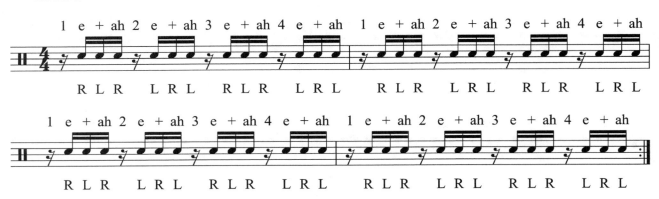

FIGURE 4-30 Sixteenth rests on downbeats and upbeats

TRACK 10

FIGURE 4-31   Random sixteenth rests

TRACK 11

The final exercise in this chapter, **FIGURE 4-31**, also uses **FIGURE 4-22** as its foundation. However, sixteenth rests are now added randomly throughout. They occur only on downbeats and upbeats, but in order to play accurately, you should play slowly and count very carefully. As with the other rhythmic examples in this chapter, refer to the CD for help.

You have now been introduced to basic duple rhythmic patterns. Duple means that every rhythm presented here is divisible by two. The figures presented here have been designed to be challenging but not impossible. It should take you—at the very least—a couple of weeks to learn to play all the rhythms in **FIGURES 4-14** through **4-30**. If it takes a month or more, that is okay, too. We all learn at different paces. Just be diligent and regular in your practice. For example, if you practice two days then take two weeks off, the two days you did practice will mean little or nothing. Retention is based on repetition.

Finally, don't be in a rush to get to the next chapter. Gradually and carefully build your confidence with each exercise. The better you grasp and perform the exercises in this chapter, the better your chances of success are in the next chapter. Everything presented in this book is cumulative. Good luck and have fun practicing!

Chapter 5

Music Reading Practice

It's time to apply your skills. Etudes allow you to gauge your progress and to test your current ability. The following study pieces will help you to build a repertoire and pinpoint both the strengths and the weaknesses in your playing. Practice each etude as if you were preparing for a recital. By doing this, the instructional value of each piece will be greatly increased.

Etude #1

Etude #1 is the simplest of the four pieces and it is designed to help you solidify your comprehension of quarter notes, eighth notes, quarter rests, eighth rests, and half notes. Half notes were not included in any of the figures in Chapter 4, but you won't have a difficult time playing them.

A half note will be played no differently than a quarter note/quarter rest combination. (See **FIGURE 5-1**.)

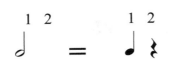

Both the half note and the quarter note/quarter rest combination equal two beats. The first beat contains a sound, while the second beat is left silent. Other instrumentalists are taught to sustain, or hold, a half note for two full counts. A trumpeter, for example, creates this sustain by blowing into his horn for two beats. A drummer cannot sustain a note unless he or she rolls. When no roll is written, drummers think of half notes as quarter note/quarter rest combinations. The same general concept is applied to whole notes as well.

The Sections of Etude #1

Etude #1 has three sections and each one has been labeled A, B, or C respectively. Each section is sixteen measures long and is repeated to allow you extra practice. You will notice that the etude takes a "breath" every four measures. This breath is due to phrasing. A segment of music that exists in between breaths is called a phrase.

A phrase either begins with a new rhythmical idea or the repeat of a previous musical idea. A phrase always ends with a small breath or musical resolution of some kind. As a beginner, it may be difficult for you to hear these rhythmical cadences, but as you gain experience, you will start noticing them. You may even begin to actually breathe with the music. This is a good thing!

Each section in Etude #1 is repeated, but, unlike the figures in Chapter 4, you will not go back to the beginning unless you are repeating section A. When repeating B or C, make sure you repeat back to the beginning of each section. You will notice that there is a start repeat sign indicated at the top of each section. Do not drop any beats when moving from the end of a section to the beginning of a section. The music must always sound seamless.

If You Run into Trouble

If you have difficulty with the rhythms in Etude #1, or any of these etudes, you may need to go back to Chapter 4 and review. You may also need to divide the etude into smaller pieces then gradually link it back together again. A typical breakdown would include practicing each bar individually, then learning two-bar snippets, followed by four-bar phrases, eight-bar phrases, and then the full section. The final step would be to play the entire etude without stopping. If you fail at this, back up a step or two and follow the same procedure until you can play the music accurately and without hesitation.

All of the etudes in this chapter are labeled "quarter note equals 120." This means that there are 120 beats per minute. If we changed the number to 60, you would play at the same speed as a second hand on a clock.

Tempo can also affect your success. March tempo (120) is indicated in the music, but this is only a suggestion. If you need to slow down, by all means, do so. Music is not a horse race. Drummers tend to value speed too much. One of the objectives of drumming is to develop velocity, but this should not be the *only* goal or even the most important goal. Reading music accurately and keeping solid time far outranks speed.

Make sure that you count off and count as you play. Maintain a steady tempo, alternate your hands, strike the drum using the correct techniques and strokes, and refer to the CD for assistance. Finally, the last note of this etude contains an accent, as shown in **FIGURES 5-2** and **5-3**. An accent tells you to strike the drum louder.

FIGURE 5-2
Accent

FIGURE 5-3

TRACK 12

Etude #1

By Eric Starr

Etude #2

Etude #2 focuses again on quarter notes and eighth notes. It is structured in three parts and each section is sixteen measures long, followed by a repeat sign. Rhythmically, there is not a huge disparity between Etude #1 and Etude #2 except that eighth rests are used more freely in the latter.

Dynamics

Your main challenge with Etude #2 will be to play the correct dynamics. Dynamic markings are volume indicators. They add expression, depth, tension, and release to music. Dynamics help to shape the notes you play by bringing out the breaths at the end of phrases. They also add forward momentum to what otherwise might sound repetitive or static.

Dynamics are spelled out using letters. The letters are abbreviations for the Italian words for *loud, soft, moderately loud, moderately soft,* and so on. Dynamic markings are written under the staff and affect the volume of the music . . . that is until another dynamic marking comes along and replaces it.

If only one dynamic has been written at the beginning of a piece, it is assumed that you would play the entire work at this volume. That's assuming that you're reading the music very strictly. Sometimes music is devoid of dynamic markings altogether, but performers take it upon themselves to add them where they see fit. For instance, the famous baroque composer J. S. Bach never wrote dynamics, but performers typically add some dynamic flair to his music.

The Most Important Dynamic Markings	
ff	fortissimo (very loud)
f	forte (loud)
m*f*	mezzo-forte (moderately loud)
mp	mezzo-piano (moderately soft)
p	piano (soft)
pp	pianissimo (very soft)

FIGURE 5-5

FIGURE 5-5 *continued*

When you play a piece of music with a lot of dynamic indicators, be certain to maintain a consistent layering of sound. For example, all ***ff*** markings should sound the same; all **mp** markings should sound the same, and so on.

Crescendos and Decrescendos

Crescendos and decrescendos, shown in **FIGURE 5-4**, are also very important. A crescendo tells you to gradually get louder. A decrescendo (sometimes called a diminuendo) tells to you gradually get softer. Turn the volume knob up and down on a stereo system. Do so very slowly and deliberately.

FIGURE 5-4
Crescendo and decrescendo

By doing this, you will hear what crescendos and decrescendos should sound like. They are not sudden changes in volume; they are slow but steady dynamic shifts.

How to Interpret Dynamic Markings

Dynamics are relative and comparative; markings on a page are only indications of the composer's intent. There is no clearly defined volume assigned to each dynamic. It is up to you to define what each dynamic will mean in a given situation.

There are several factors to consider and each one of them revolves around your musical environment. For example, pianissimo for an

FIGURE 5-6

Etude #3

By Eric Starr

FIGURE 5-6 *continued*

orchestral drummer and pianissimo for a rock drummer mean two very different things. The orchestral drummer's pianissimo would be played whisper soft. The rock drummer's pianissimo would probably be played quite loud; it might even equal the orchestral drummer's mezzo-forte.

The musicians that you are playing with also affect dynamic choices. If you are playing with a standup bass player, you will need to be mindful of how loudly you play, especially if that bass player is not using an amplifier. If you are playing with a rock guitarist who has turned his Marshall stack up to eleven, you will be free to really pound on your drums. In fact, you'll need to!

Acoustics

Finally, room acoustics affect dynamic choices. If you are playing in a reverberant auditorium, you may want to reduce your fortes and fortissimos. If you are playing in a room with no echo or reverberation, you may choose to explore dynamic extremes. The only ironclad rule with dynamics is to always use your ears when you play and, if you're playing with other musicians, never overpower them. Try playing Etude #2 in **FIGURE 5-5**.

Etude #3

Etude #3 (**FIGURE 5-6**) uses sixteenth notes and an abundance of dynamic markings. This etude is longer than the previous two etudes. You will notice that there is an additional sixteen-bar section marked D tagged on at the end.

Practice using the same methods you used in Etude #1 and #2. In other words, learn the music in segments, then gradually link bars together until you form the whole piece. If you are having trouble playing the notes, accents, and dynamics, learn the notes first. After you feel comfortable playing the rhythms, you can go back and add the accents and dynamics to the music. Don't forget to alternate your sticks in a right-left or left-right fashion and carefully observe each repeat.

Etude #4

Etude #4 also has four sections. Again, you will see copious use of sixteenth notes, but now you have been asked to deal with sixteenth rests, too.

There are a few new elements you need to know about before you begin. First and second endings have to do with the way a passage of music is repeated. (See **FIGURE 5-7**.) As you might have guessed, a first ending refers to the first time you play through a given section. A second ending refers to the second time through that same section. Be careful

FIGURE 5-7
First and second endings

not to take the first ending by mistake when you're on the second time through the section. Sections A and C both use first and second endings.

In section B, you will notice that there is a new dynamic marking. It is **s ƒ z**. This dynamic stands for *sforzando*. This means to play a sudden, loud accent followed by an equally sudden drop in volume. You will also notice that there are three **mp** dynamics used, and on the very last note, you are asked to play one **ƒ ƒƒ** dynamic; **ƒ ƒƒ** stands for *forte-fortissimo*. You can probably guess what this means: Hit the drum extremely loud!

Lastly, there is a D.C. al fine (feen-ay) used in this piece. D.C. stands for Da capo. Translated, *Da capo al fine* means "the head to the end." After you finish section D, go back to A, then take the second ending. Repeats are not observed on a D.C., so don't play the first ending this time around.

Most of the advice given in this chapter really applies to all four etudes. General comments written about Etude #1, for example, apply to Etude #4 (**FIGURE 5-8**) as well. If you're patient but hard working, all of these etudes should be well within your grasp. Remember, everything is cumulative, so learn these etudes in numeric order and do not move on to the next piece until you're really ready. Don't accept shoddy renditions of these etudes from yourself. Make them sound just like the recording!

FIGURE 5-8

TRACK 15

Etude #4

By Eric Starr

FIGURE 5-8 *continued*

Chapter 6

Building
Technique

This chapter deals with the nitty-gritty of drum technique. Rudiments are the most important technique-building exercises used by drummers and you will need to practice them for as long as you play the instrument. Indeed, rudiments should be part of your daily practice regimen.

What Are Rudiments?

Rudiments are a collection of rhythm and sticking exercises used to develop hand technique. Rudiments are the building blocks of stick control. You can think of them as scales for drums. A saxophonist, for example, must know major and minor scales like the back of his or her hand. Your relationship with rudiments must be the same.

The History of Rudiments

Rudiments are rooted in military history. They were first developed by the Swiss in the fourteenth century and eventually found their way over to France and Britain. During the Revolutionary War, British drummers introduced rudiments to Americans.

By the 1800s, a number of instructional manuals were written on the subject in the United States but it wasn't until the 1930s that rudiments appeared in their modern form.

When rudiments first originated, there was no standard of notation. To make matters worse, in the eighteenth, nineteenth, and early twentieth centuries, arguments ensued over the "right" way to play them. In 1933, this was all put to rest when thirteen of the most prominent American drummers of the day convened at the American Legion National Convention in Chicago, Illinois. They called themselves the National Association of Rudimental Drummers (NARD), and their purpose was to standardize a list of rudiments for those who wished to join their organization. This list did more than inform prospective NARD members, it quelled regional disputes and became the rudimental bible for all American drummers. This list is still used today!

NARD and PAS

NARD came up with two important categories: the Thirteen Essential Rudiments and the Twenty-six Standard American Drum Rudiments. The latter was comprised of thirteen additional, or as they called them, "auxiliary," rudiments.

By the mid to late 1900s, drumming had evolved more into a civilian art form and the drum set became the most popular percussion instrument. Soon, drummers began to feel that additional rudiments were needed to meet the demands of a changing musical world. By the late twentieth century, the Percussive Arts Society (PAS) stepped up to the challenge and compiled a list of rudiments that included NARD's twenty-six, plus fourteen new ones.

PAS's list was the result of five years of research by an international rudimental committee comprised of select percussionists from around the globe. As of this writing, PAS's list stands as the most accepted catalog of rudiments available to drummers. Over the years this list will continue to grow. In fact, other publications and Web sites already boast new rudiments. You can take part in this, too. After you've learned PAS's forty, feel free to make up your own list of rudiments and have fun practicing and sharing them with other drummers.

This book does not cover every rudiment from the NARD or PAS list. Refer to Appendix B to find out how to obtain more information on this subject.

Rudiments for Beginners

As a beginner, you will need to focus on the "big three" rudiments. They are:

- The single stroke roll.
- The double stroke roll (long roll).
- The single paradiddle.

Many of the NARD and PAS rudiments are rooted in these three granddaddy rudiments. Before we discuss the "big three," you need to know how to practice them. You should first always check your grip and hand position, and use only the strokes previously described in this book. Second, do not deviate from the indicated stickings. Sticking is one of the most significant features of rudiments. Third, do not be in a hurry to play fast. It takes time to develop velocity. Sticking precision and rhythmical accuracy are more important.

Always focus on the hand you lead, or start, with. If you find that your leading hand switches while you're playing, you need to stop and start again at a slower speed. The golden rule here is to make sure you begin and end with the same hand. If your hands get tangled up, that means that somewhere along the way you dropped a beat or a part of a beat.

Finally, when practicing a rudiment, or any exercise for that matter, loop the pattern until you feel comfortable with it. You'll notice that many of the following exercises are written with a repeat sign at the end. Don't take this literally. Repeat each figure over and over until you feel that you've made progress. You may find yourself playing a rudiment for five or ten minutes!

Single Stroke Roll

The single stroke roll uses the same alternating sticking pattern that you learned in Chapter 3. You've been playing a slow version of the single stroke roll and didn't even know it. **FIGURE 6-1** shows it written using thirty-second notes.

Thirty-second notes are nothing to be nervous about. They look tough but they aren't demanding on their own. Any difficulty lies in the tempo you choose. Thirty-second notes are played twice the speed of sixteenth notes and follow the same 1:2 relationship that was described in Chapter 4.

FIGURE 6-1 Single stroke roll

TRACK 16

Practicing Single Stroke Rolls

The single stroke roll should be practiced open-closed-open. This means that you start very slow, then gradually increase the tempo until the roll sounds like a long, sustained note. When you reach your peak speed, hold the tempo steady for ten to fifteen seconds then gradually release it. Moving from open to closed to open should take about a minute, and, again, your transitions should be very gradual.

FIGURE 6-2
Thumbs-up
position

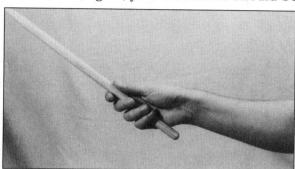

A single stroke roll played fast sounds a lot like machine-gun fire. You will use a half stroke at this speed, and for ultrafast tempos, you will need to turn your fingers in a thumbs-up position to gain velocity. Once in this position, you will propel the sticks by grasping them with fulcrum A and rapidly tapping your index, ring, and pinkie fingers on the stick shafts. (See **FIGURE 6-2**.)

Single Stroke Rhythmic Variations

Sometimes drummers use other exercises to increase their rudimental skill. The single stroke roll is particularly difficult to maintain at fast clips, so rhythmic variations can be used to address this problem.

In **FIGURE 6-3** you will see three single stroke exercises. The purpose of these patterns is to help you acclimate to fast speeds. As previously stated, it's very difficult to maintain a lightning-fast roll for long durations, but if you use short spurts, you can eventually gain control of breakneck speeds without tensing up or falling apart altogether.

The exercise in **FIGURE 6-4** is very similar to **FIGURE 6-3** except that you will play longer thirty-second note spurts.

This next exercise can be altered to fit just about any sticking. It also represents a different approach to learning the big three rudiments as we will discuss later in the chapter. **FIGURE 6-5** shifts from slow to fast in distinct, measured jumps. We will call this approach the "step" method since it uses a 1:2 rhythmic division to shift from slow to fast to slow again. Using this method, the tempo always remains intact and there are no accelerandos (speedups) or ritardandos (slowdowns).

FIGURE 6-3   Single stroke using short spurts

* Practice leading with the left too!

FIGURE 6-4   Single stroke using longer spurts

*Practice with leading with the left too!

FIGURE 6-5 Single stroke using "step method"

* Practice leading with the left too!

It's important that you never lose the 1:2 relationships between notes. To increase your success rate, subdivide the quarter notes as you count. If you don't subdivide, you may end up playing quarter notes as eighth notes by mistake. Remember, to subdivide means to count quarter notes in terms of sixteenth notes. You will play only on the downbeats, but you will count "one-e-and-ah, two-e-and-ah, three-e-and-ah, four-e-and-ah."

Double Stroke Roll

This rudiment is commonly referred to as the long roll. Older generations used to refer to it affectionately as the "mama-dada" rudiment. This phrase connects with students because when said aloud, it sounds a lot like the double stroke roll itself. Our old friend onomatopoeia is at work here again. (See **FIGURE 6-6**.)

We can use "mama-dada" to learn about the double stroke roll. You'll see that this phrase has four syllables, just as one cycle of the long roll contains four notes. The long roll also has two parts, just like mama-dada. Also, both mama-dada and the long roll are symmetrical. The double stroke roll is made up of two rights and two lefts. Similarly, mama-dada contains two syllables per word.

FIGURE 6-6   Double stroke roll

TRACK 17

Typically, this roll is taught using the open-closed-open approach. In the closed position, it should have a machine-gun effect similar to the single stroke roll.

What Is a Closed Roll?

There is some dispute over what closed means in drumming. Some contend that a closed roll is equivalent to a buzz roll. Others claim that *closed* simply refers to the peak speed, not necessarily a change in the amount of notes played in one cycle.

What's the difference? A double stroke roll uses two, and only two, notes per hand. The buzz roll uses multiple bounces. When playing the latter, each hand plays four to six very tight bounces, creating a buzzing sound.

Orchestral drummers commonly use buzz rolls because it has a smooth, refined tone. Because of this, the buzz roll is often referred to as an *orchestral roll.* On the other hand, marching drummers never use the buzz roll. They maintain a strict double stroke at all times. Drum set players use both freely.

You will enjoy choosing the rolls that best fit the music you play. For now, do not confuse or combine the double stroke roll with the buzz roll, as this will only interfere in your technique building. And when you play the closed portion of the roll, always use doubles.

Proper Technique

Learning the proper way to execute a double stroke roll requires hard work and patience. You will not learn how to play this roll overnight. In fact, it could take you months. But be optimistic and gauge your progress by recording your roll once a week. Compare each recording and critique your work as you see fit.

As previously stated, when you play a long roll, you will play two notes per hand. The first note is called the primary stroke. The second note, not surprisingly, is called the secondary stroke. Your work with the whole and half strokes will come into play a great deal here.

After you play the primary stroke, allow your stick to rebound. The second note should be the result of the bounce, not a forced wrist movement. If you hear an accent on the primary stroke, this is okay. Later, you will learn—quite naturally—how to play this roll with an even dynamic. You will even learn, with a little practice, how to accentuate the secondary note. This will occur after you've developed finger technique.

In the first stages, practice slow, even double strokes and think *snap-bounce* as you strike the drum. Don't worry about playing the open-closed-open approach just yet. Concentrate on the snap-bounce feel. Use your wrist for the primary stroke snap. After the secondary bounce, gently cup your fingers around the stick to stop it from bouncing again.

Increasing Your Speed

As you gain proficiency with this, you can begin to increase your speed. When doing so, keep the pulse and the space in between the primary and secondary strokes even and articulate. You do not want the roll to sound like a bag of marbles falling down a stairwell. When you increase speed, you will not need to cup your fingers around the stick to stop it from bouncing multiple times. Leave the stick in motion and guide it with a wrist/finger combination.

Playing a roll at fast speed is like playing a game of paddleball. Remember Newton's Third Law: For every action there is a reaction. Don't interfere in this natural movement. Put the stick into motion and guide it with your wrists and fingers.

To propel the sticks faster, use your fingers as you did with the single stroke roll. The only difference is that you shouldn't put your hands in a thumbs-up position. You need to use a combination of wrists and fingers to play the double stroke roll, so put your hands in a position that is halfway between the palm-flat and thumbs-up positions. By doing this, you will get the full range of motion needed in both your wrists and fingers.

Now let's take **FIGURE 6-6** and rewrite it using the double-stroke sticking. As before, we'll refer to this as the "step" method. The step method will improve your sense of rhythmic relationships, reinforce the hand techniques spelled out previously, and improve your sense of time. See **FIGURE 6-7**.

Lastly, **FIGURE 6-8** is an advanced double stroke roll variation. You should not attempt this until you can play the traditional long roll. In the following exercise, you will see that accents have been added to the secondary strokes. By bringing out the secondary strokes, you will develop more articulate finger control.

FIGURE 6-7 Double stroke using step method

* Practice leading with the left too!

FIGURE 6-8 Double stroke accenting secondary strokes

Single Paradiddle

The single paradiddle (**FIGURE 6-9**) combines the single stroke roll with the double stroke roll. Its name, not surprisingly, also stems from onomatopoeia. If you say *paradiddle* out loud, you will hear the relationship between the word and the sound of the rudiment.

You will notice that the paradiddle uses a single-stroke sticking on the first half of the pattern and a double-stroke sticking on the second half of the pattern. The cycle is eight notes long and accents appear on the first and fifth notes. This rudiment uses a snap-tap-bounce-bounce technique. The snap is made with the wrists, the opposing hand makes the tap, and

FIGURE 6-9   Single paradiddle

TRACK 18

FIGURE 6-10   Single paradiddle using step method

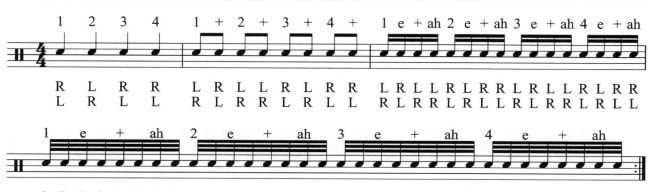

the bounce-bounce is the result of a proper grip and fulcrum. You should practice this rudiment using both the open-closed-open approach and the step method. **FIGURE 6-5** has been rewritten with a single paradiddle substitution to create **FIGURE 6-10**.

Combining What You Know

Once you gain proficiency with the big three rudiments, try combining them together in a single exercise. Following, you will see that a four-bar exercise has been written. It begins with singles, then moves to doubles, and then to two measures of single paradiddles. You will notice that the accents have been omitted from the single paradiddle. This is done to create a consistency of sound. Try to make the sixteenths notes sound as even and flowing as possible. In other words, the listener should not notice a change in sticking. This exercise should sound like you're hitting the drum with one hand. **FIGURE 6-11** is very difficult and should be focused on only after you've gained considerable progress with each individual rudiment.

Once you feel comfortable with **FIGURE 6-11**, try changing the sticking order. Maybe you will play one measure of paradiddles, one measure of single strokes, and two measures of double strokes. There are a number of permutations at your disposal. You decide!

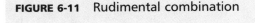

FIGURE 6-11 Rudimental combination

*R L R L R L R L R L R L R L R L   R R L L R R L L R R L L R R L L

R L R R L R L L R L R R L R L L   R L R R L R L L R L R R L R L L

*Practice leading with the left too!

Open-Closed-Open versus Step

Some instructors have abandoned the traditional open-closed-open approach to teaching the big three rudiments. Instead, they ask their students to use the so-called step method. Often this method is accompanied by strict practice with a metronome. Some teachers contend that the open-closed-open method encourages rushing and dragging and that this will have a negative effect on a student's overall sense of time.

ALERT!

Never practice on a soft surface such as a pillow. Many teachers and books advocate this approach, claiming that pillow practice strengthens your hands and fingers. This method also promotes overexertion, forced and wasted motion, and stiff playing. You're not in training to be a "pillower." Practice on drums or well-designed pads.

The step method is, undoubtedly, more practical. It promotes rhythmical understanding, and good timekeeping. However, what its promoters don't tell you is that the open-closed-open method allows the student to momentarily set aside issues of time and concentrate on technique alone. In this sense, history has shown the open-closed-open approach to be both efficient and effective. The important thing is to know its role. The open-closed-open method should be used only as an approach to building technique. It should not be confused with issues pertaining to timekeeping.

Once you learn how to control wrist snaps, bounces, and fingers, you should regularly practice both the open-closed-open method and the step method. This way you will benefit from both schools of thought.

In summary, always consider yourself a student of rudiments. All serious drummers practice and review rudiments, just as all pianists, guitarists, and other pitched instrumentalists run scales. This applies to professionals and amateurs alike. (E)

Chapter 7

Other Key Rudiments

Before we delve into more etudes, you will need to know some of the other key rudiments. You've already learned the big three rudiments. Now you must expand your rudimental skill. The only way to do this is to gradually work your way through all forty PAS rudiments. In this chapter, we will concentrate on some of the more important ones.

Double Stroke Roll Rudiments

The double stroke roll is the king of the rudimental jungle. It has many variations, and some of them can be tricky because they require beginning and ending on opposite hands. All of these rolls are important, so every one of them from the PAS list is included here.

Make sure that you play only double strokes. You can play these rolls using buzzes, but for now, stick only to doubles. A double stroke or long roll has no specific ending; the following rolls do have specific endings. What is the application? They are practical versions of the long roll. Observe the rhythmic quality of each roll. These rolls are used to replace or adorn otherwise plain note combinations.

Five Stroke Roll

The five stroke roll, like each roll that follows, is a fragment or snippet of the long roll. (See **FIGURE 7-1**.) You will play two sets of double strokes and end with a single stroke. In music, it will most commonly take the place of two eighth notes. Therefore, it has been notated as such. Often, drummers count the primary strokes in order to avoid confusion. You never want to ask yourself, "How long did I just play that roll?"

With the five stroke roll, you will count to three. Make sure you alternate when you practice. When referring to rolls, to alternate means to play the roll leading with your left or right hand, then begin the next roll with the opposite hand. For example, start and end with the right hand, then start and end with the left hand.

FIGURE 7-1 Five stroke roll

TRACK 19

Six Stroke Roll

The six stroke roll is quite fancy and very useful when filling or soloing. It can be notated and played two different ways. The unusual aspect of this roll is the use of single strokes. You will notice that in version A, the roll ends with two single strokes played as sixteenth notes. In version B, the roll begins with a single stroke and ends with a single stroke. Version A commonly replaces the eighth/two sixteenths pattern. Version B would replace a dotted eighth/sixteenth pattern.

Dotted notes stretch or add time to note values. If you place a dot next to a note, that note will be stretched half its own value. For example, if you have a dotted quarter note, that note will be worth 1½ beats (a quarter plus an eighth). The quarter note eats up one beat and the dot adds what amounts to an eighth rest to the total value of the quarter note.

It works the same way with eighth notes. If you add a dot to an eighth note, the dot will be equal to a sixteenth rest, making the eighth note's total value equal ¾ of a beat (½ of a beat plus ¼ of a beat equals ¾ of a beat).

It sounds more complicated than it really is. Refer to the previous notation and/or to Chapter 4 if you need to review the fractional backbone of notation. To simplify things, subdivide the beat. In other words, count the dotted eighth/sixteenth pattern in terms of sixteenth notes. Count: "one-e-and-ah, two-e-and-ah, three-e-and-ah, four-e-and-ah." The eighth note and the dot take the place of the *one-e-and* but not the *ah*. The *one* and the *ah* are your single strokes. When counting primary strokes for the six stroke roll, you will count to four. (See **FIGURES 7-2** and **7-3**.)

FIGURE 7-2 Six stroke roll A with primary strokes indicated   **FIGURE 7-3** Six stroke roll B

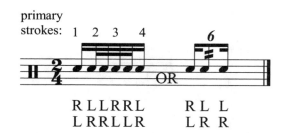

Seven Stroke Roll

Some of the odd-numbered rolls will begin and end on opposite hands. You should practice leading with both hands, but don't get confused. If you start with the right hand, you will end with the left hand. If you start with the left hand, you will end with the right hand. Do not alternate hands midway. The hand you lead with will be the hand you consistently lead with until you stop playing. Once you stop, you may resume leading with another hand.

Like the five stroke roll, the seven stroke roll (**FIGURE 7-4**) commonly replaces two eighth notes. Therefore, it has been notated as such. If you count the primary strokes, you will count to four.

Nine Stroke Roll

The nine stroke roll (**FIGURE 7-5**) is a double five stroke roll. It replaces two quarter notes, though the second quarter note is not rolled on; it is only the final downbeat of the roll. Make sure that you alternate (as delineated previously) when you practice this roll. If you count the primary strokes, you will count to five.

Ten Stroke Roll

The ten stroke roll (**FIGURE 7-6**), like the seven stroke roll, begins on one hand and ends on the opposite hand. Like the six stroke, it uses two single strokes. You will not alternate when you play this roll. However,

FIGURE 7-4 Seven stroke roll

TRACK 21

FIGURE 7-5 Nine stroke roll

TRACK 22

make sure you practice leading with both hands. Typically, the ten stroke roll replaces a quarter note/two sixteenths pattern as previously notated. If you count primary strokes, you will count to six.

Eleven Stroke Roll

The eleven stroke roll (**FIGURE 7-7**) is the brother to the ten stroke roll. In fact, they are exactly the same, except for the penultimate, or second to last, stroke. On this stroke, you will play a double stroke rather than a single stroke. If you count primary strokes, you will count to six.

Thirteen Stroke Roll

The thirteen stroke roll (**FIGURE 7-8**) begins and ends with the same hand, so therefore you will alternate. It typically replaces a quarter

FIGURE 7-6   Ten stroke roll

TRACK 23

primary strokes: 1 2 3 4 5 6   *10*

RRLLRRLL R L   R RL
LLRRLLRR L R   L LR

FIGURE 7-7   Eleven stroke roll

TRACK 24

primary strokes: 1 2 3 4 5 6   *11*

RRLLRRLLRRL   R RL
LLRRLLRRLLR   L LR

FIGURE 7-8   Thirteen stroke roll

TRACK 25

primary strokes: 1   2   3   4   5   6   7   *13*

R L L R L L R L L R L L R   R   R   R
L L R R L L L R R L L R R L   L   L   L

note/two eighths combination. If you count primary strokes, you will count to seven.

Fifteen Stroke Roll

The fifteen stroke roll (**FIGURE 7-9**) begins and ends with opposite hands, so therefore you will not alternate. It typically replaces a quarter note/dotted eighth/sixteenth combination. If you count primary strokes, you will count to eight.

Seventeen Stroke Roll

Like the five, nine, and thirteen stroke rolls, you will begin and end the seventeen stroke roll (**FIGURE 7-10**) with the same hand you started with. Therefore, you will alternate when practicing this roll. The seventeen

FIGURE 7-9 Fifteen stroke roll

TRACK 26

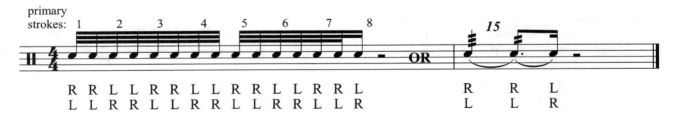

FIGURE 7-10 Seventeen stroke roll

TRACK 27

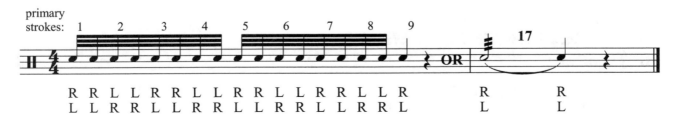

stroke roll commonly replaces a half note/quarter note combination. If you count primary strokes, you will count to nine.

Once you learn these nine double stroke rolls you will know the full catalog of this roll type. We could keep going with twenty-one stroke rolls, twenty-five stroke rolls, and so on, but this is not necessary. Rolls of longer durations are merely combinations of the rolls notated previously.

The Flam

The flam is not a roll, but rather, a fancier way to play any given note. Flams adorn whole, half, quarter, eighth, and sixteenth notes. Flams make notes more interesting and colorful, adding both depth and breadth to a note. Flams are made up of main notes and grace notes. (See **FIGURE 7-11**.) The main note is the counted note. Counted notes include quarter notes, eighth notes, sixteenth notes, and so on. The grace note is not counted. It is a soft tap that is played just prior to the main note. When played properly, the two notes are placed almost on top of each other. You must be careful not to play them as double stops or "flat flams," though.

FIGURE 7-11   The flam

TRACK 28

A double stop would mean that the two notes are played precisely at the same time. This is not the case with flams. Like so many other rudiments, onomatopoeia should help you to understand this rudiment. Say *flam* out loud. This word has two syllables. If we spell it phonetically, it would be spelled "fa-lam." The *fa* represents the grace note, and the *lam* represents the main note. If you play the notes on top of each other, you will not get a *fa-lam* sound. Instead, you will hear an ugly popping sound, as the drumhead gets choked by the two sticks.

Stick placement is very important when practicing flams. You will have to use control strokes to play this rudiment properly. A control stoke refers to down and upstrokes which were mentioned briefly in Chapter 3. When you use a control stroke, you will need to interfere with the natural trajectory of the stick by rejecting the bounce. By doing this, you will be able to position your sticks exactly as you desire.

When playing a right-handed flam, point your right hand in an "up" position. This means that the tip of the stick will point straight at the ceiling. Next, place your left stick about 1" above the drumhead or pad. When you drop the sticks onto the drum, the left hand will naturally strike first, as it has only 1" to move, versus the right hand, which must traverse about a foot.

After you strike the drum, your hands do two different things. The left hand will tap the drum softly, then be raised to an up position. The right hand will strike the drum, then be raised only about 1"; this is called a down stroke. In essence, you will be playing an upstroke followed quickly by a down stroke. This will place the right hand in the proper position to play the grace note for a left flam and the left hand in the proper position to play a main note. The role reversal of the sticks gives you the ability to alternate.

You will want to practice flams in the alternating pattern as previously notated. Make sure you always maintain the proper stick positions, and listen carefully to the sound you're making on each flam. You never want to "pop" the flam. Conversely, you don't want to space the two flam notes too far apart, either. If you do, the grace note will sound like a soft main note. Listen to the CD as a reference.

If you wish to play flams at softer dynamics, simply lower the position of the hand you've chosen to play the main note. You can also slightly lower the hand you've chosen to play the grace note. You must, however, always maintain a healthy spread between the sticks. Never place the sticks at the same height. If you do, you'll run the risk of popping your flams.

When you play a right flam, always strike the drum first with your left hand. When you play a left flam, always strike the drum first with your right hand.

The Drag

The drag is also commonly called a three-stroke ruff (**FIGURE 7-12**). This rudiment is very similar to the flam because it uses both grace notes and main notes. You will also use the exact same hand positioning that was described previously. Moreover, the role of the drag is similar to that of the flam.

The difference between the flam and the drag lies in the use of grace notes. With the drag, you will now play two grace notes and one main note. These grace notes will be subtle, soft bounces. Make sure you do not buzz the grace notes. You should hear three distinct notes. The first two notes should be heard faintly; the third note should be accented. Make sure you alternate as you practice this rudiment and listen to the CD to hear how it should sound.

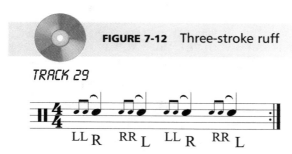

FIGURE 7-12   Three-stroke ruff

TRACK 29

Double Paradiddle

The double paradiddle is the sister to the single paradiddle. The only difference is that the double paradiddle contains two additional single-stroke stickings. This is why some people refer to this rudiment as the *paraparadiddle.* Again, you can see the onomatopoeia at work here. (See **FIGURE 7-13**.)

This rudiment can be tricky because it crosses over the beat. Its irregular form means that the double paradiddle is worth a beat and a half in 4/4. It is most commonly found in 6/8 music, however, and this is the way it has been written in this text. (For more on 6/8, see

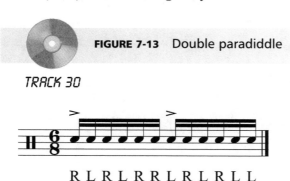

FIGURE 7-13   Double paradiddle

TRACK 30

Chapter 16.) When playing this rudiment, don't forget to place an accent at the beginning of each paraparadiddle.

Of course, follow the sticking closely. This is a real stick twister!

The Buzz or Multiple Bounce Roll

Assuming that you now know the double stroke roll and its derivatives, it's time to learn the buzz roll. If you're just skimming through this book, do not attempt to play a buzz roll without first learning the double stroke roll. In the long run, you'll do yourself a favor. Why? You won't be tempted to skip the double stroke roll altogether.

You'll find that gaining proficiency with the buzz roll is a lot easier than gaining proficiency with the long roll. Don't take the path of least resistance. Some students cop out, figuring that they can "get away with" the buzz in most musical situations. Don't let this be you. The buzz is not to be confused with the novelty roll, the press roll. The press roll uses abnormally tight buzzes. In fact, they're so tight, that the roll sounds purposely ugly. For this reason, the press roll should be used only sparingly. Sometimes it's effective in jazz, but you should not worry about it at this stage in the game.

When playing a buzz roll, you must make each buzz really sing. Practice playing using each hand individually before you try putting them together to create the roll. After you learn how to play individual buzzes, connect them together so that as one buzz begins to decay, you play another buzz with the alternate hand. What you're actually playing are buzzed sixteenth notes. When the roll is properly executed, it should sound smooth and refined. This type of roll is the closest a drummer can get to sustain.

FIGURE 7-14
Buzz roll

TRACK 31

The buzz roll (**FIGURE 7-14**) heard on the CD begins with individual buzzes played alternately between hands. Gradually, each buzz is sped up until you hear the buzz roll in its complete form. Like double stroke rolls, a buzz will always end with single stroke.

Other Helpful Exercises

One of the most helpful groups of exercises revolves around working your hands individually. This approach has long been preached by great teachers such as Billy Gladstone, Joe Morello, Roy Burns, and others. The idea is simple; the effects are remarkable.

The belief is that if you develop strong finger and wrist control with each hand individually, when you put them together to form rolls or other complex rhythms, your ability to play accurately will be greatly improved and you will be able to play faster.

First, practice using only the wrist. After you feel comfortable doing this, practice holding the sticks with fulcrum A and tapping your fingers on the shaft of the stick the same way you would when playing a single stroke roll. Allow the sticks to bounce freely on the drumhead. When doing this, you will need to put your hands in a thumbs-up position.

Don't push the tempo beyond your means. Always play at a speed where you can still retain control of the sticks. If you go too fast, you will find that you get fatigued and tense. Speed should come naturally through a steady diet of practice. Try playing **FIGURE 7-15**.

FIGURE 7-15 Technique-building exercise

FIGURE 7-16   Technique-building exercise

R   R   R   R   R R R R R R   L   L   L   L   L L L L L L L

R   R   R   R   R R R R R R   L   L   L   L   L L L L L L L

FIGURE 7-17   Technique-building exercise

R   R R   R R R   R R R   R R   L   L L L   L L L   L L L   L L

R   R R   R R   R R R   R R R   L L L   L L L   L L L   L L L

Now try various rhythmical combinations. **FIGURES 7-16** and **7-17** are a couple of sample exercises. Come up with your own variations, too. Have fun with this. You can take virtually any rhythmic combination (as long as it doesn't include rolls or grace notes) and practice them one hand at a time. Remember to try leading with both hands. Try leading with your weak hand for an extra-strong workout. Ⓔ

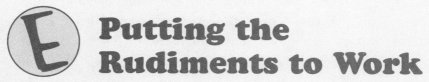

Chapter 8

Putting the Rudiments to Work

This chapter is admittedly a little tough. However, everything you will find here is very playable given the right attitude, patience, and practice. Moreover, if you've followed this book step by step, these solos should be well within your means. The solos presented here utilize the rudiments and rhythms you've been taught so far. You must be cautious and observant with each piece. Try learning each etude one section—or even one bar—at a time and be sure to refer to the CD for assistance.

Rudimental Etude #1: Bakerloo

The solo in **FIGURE 8-1** is designed to give you a thorough workout with five stroke rolls and single paradiddles. Like Etude #3 and Etude #4 in Chapter 5, the structure of "Bakerloo" is broken into four repeated sixteen-measure sections labeled A, B, C, and D respectively. Take this piece slowly at first and observe all the repeats, dynamics, and accents. Most of all, make sure you follow each sticking to the tee. Do not go on to the next etude until you have fully mastered this one.

Rudimental Etude #2: Rolling Home

This solo (see **FIGURE 8-2**) is designed to give you a thorough workout with not only the five stroke roll, but all the other PAS roll rudiments—except for the buzz roll and the triple stroke roll, the latter of which we haven't even discussed. Like "Bakerloo," this piece is broken into four repeated sixteen-measure sections labeled A, B, C, and D respectively. Play "Rolling Home" slowly at first and don't be intimidated by the notation. This piece is really just a lot of rolls strung together, especially in section C. It's very important that you do not lose track of the quarter note pulse when playing this etude.

Rudimental Etude #3: Gracie Mansion

The solo in **FIGURE 8-3** is designed to help you with grace notes, hence the play on words in the title. As you will see, this etude is broken down into four repeated sixteen-bar sections labeled A, B, C, and D respectively. You will be dealing with flams in sections A and B. In section C, you will be faced with only drags or ruffs. In section D, both flams and drags have been written in. In section B, you will see a common flam rudiment called a *flam tap,* and in section D, you will also see another common rudiment, the single-drag tap. These new rudiments shouldn't be too difficult to navigate your way around.

To make things a little easier, no dynamics have been added to this piece. However, feel free to add your own nuances and even dynamic contrasts as you become fluent with this etude. As always, go slowly at first and carefully observe each sticking.

FACT

Practice each etude as if you were going to perform it in front of an audience. In fact, these solos may be appropriate for certain auditions or competitions.

Rudimental Etude #4: Bourbon Street

This is by far the most difficult of the four etudes presented in this chapter. If this solo is too difficult, skip it for now and go on to the chapters on the drum set. However, don't give up without a fight. You *can* play this piece! It will just take a little extra time, practice, and most of all perseverance.

In order to play "Bourbon Street" at the indicated speed, you will need to develop considerable technical facility. If you're not up to the challenge, start by reviewing the exercises in Chapters 6 and 7, particularly the exercises that concentrate on individual hand development. Also, it is a good idea to make up your own technical exercises designed to target your own deficiencies. The good news is that by gaining proficiency with this piece, you will be well on your way toward advanced snare drumming. Also, you will already have procured many of the technical tools needed to play great solos on the drum set.

This piece (see **FIGURE 8-4**), unlike any other in the book, is a "through composed" work and has no specific sections or even blatant phrases. It is a motor piece designed to introduce you to the wonders of tricky sticking patterns and advanced syncopation. This said, "Bourbon Street" will enhance not only your stick control but your understanding of complex duple rhythmic patterns.

Don't be afraid of the thirty-second notes designated by the triple lines or flags. You've already been playing thirty-second notes and didn't even know it. Every time you played a double stroke roll variation in the previous etudes, you've played thirty-second notes. The thirty-second notes are written out here simply for ease in reading. Good luck and have fun with this piece! At the very least, learn each measure individually, then try getting through the entire solo at a slow but steady tempo. Any actual rolls notated here may be played as buzzes or double strokes as you wish.

FIGURE 8-1 Rudimental Etude #1—Bakerloo

TRACK 32

FIGURE 8-1 Rudimental Etude #1—Bakerloo—*continued*

FIGURE 8-2 Rudimental Etude #2—Rolling Home

FIGURE 8-2 Rudimental Etude #2—Rolling Home—*continued*

FIGURE 8-3 Rudimental Etude #3—Gracie Mansion

Gracie Mansion

By Eric Starr

FIGURE 8-3 Rudimental Etude #3—Gracie Mansion—*continued*

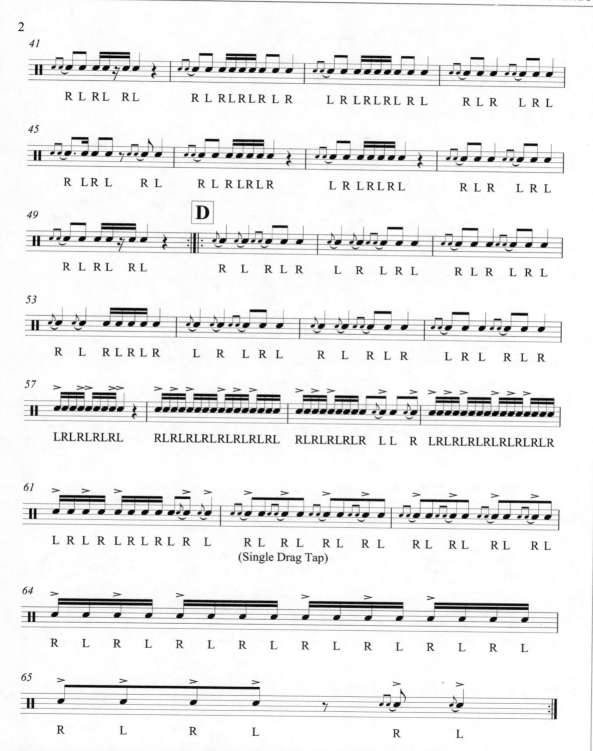

FIGURE 8-4   Rudimental Etude #4—Bourbon Street

For Andrew Lawton

Bourbon Street

By Eric Starr

FIGURE 8-4 Rudimental Etude #4—Bourbon Street—*continued*

FIGURE 8-4 Rudimental Etude #4—Bourbon Street—*continued*

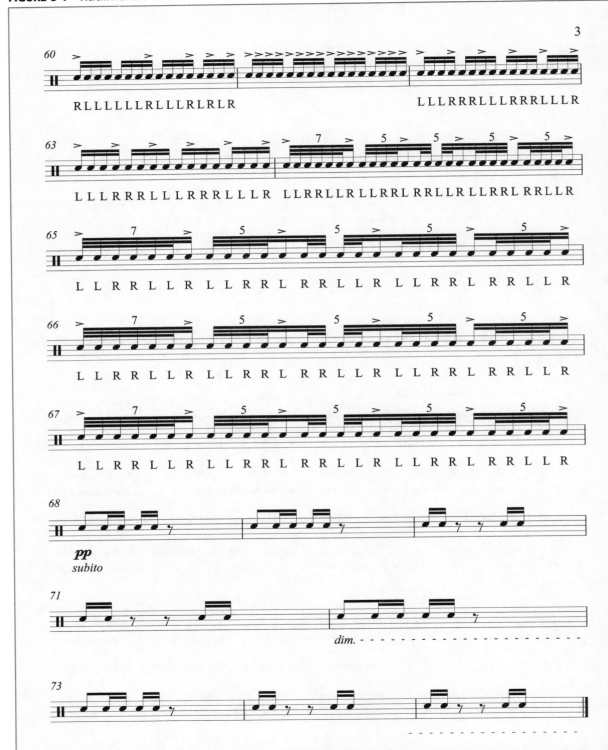

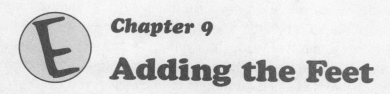

Chapter 9

Adding the Feet

It's now time to learn how to play the drum set. If you don't have a drum set, don't worry. At the end of the chapter, you will learn how you can practice without one. Before you do anything, refer back to Chapter 1 for setup information. Once your drums or drum simulations are in place, you're ready to use both your hands and your feet to create music.

Playing the Bass Drum

You will need a pedal to play the bass drum. A pedal consists of three main parts: a footboard, a beater for striking the drum, and a spring to allow the beater to move back and forth properly. When in rest position, your pedal should have enough spring tension to hold the beater at a 135-degree angle. When you press down on the pedal, you should feel some resistance but not so much that it is difficult to create a sound. If the beater does not touch the head when you press on the pedal, chances are you have forgotten to clamp the pedal securely to the bass drum's hoop. If the beater is resting on the head all by itself, you need to tighten the spring.

The Heel-Tap

There are four main techniques associated with the bass, or kick drum, as studio musicians often call it. The most fundamental pedal technique is the "heel-tap" method.

The heel-tap technique is no different than an ordinary foot tap. When you tap your foot on the floor, you do not lift your entire foot off the ground. Your heel rests on the floor and you tap the ball of your foot on the ground. The same is true with this bass drum technique; your heel will remain planted on the footboard as the ball of your foot presses

FIGURE 9-1 Bass drum exercise

FIGURE 9-2 Bass drum exercise

down on the pedal. After you strike the drum, allow the beater to spring back naturally. Do not press the beater into the drum then leave it touching the head.

After the beater springs back, make sure that you do not raise your foot higher than the resting point of the pedal itself. In other words, the bottom of your foot should be in contact with the footboard at all times. The pedal should seem like the sole of your shoe. Try playing quarter notes then eighth notes using this method and always keep your ankle, foot, and toes relaxed. Once you've gained some control playing quarters and eighths, try adding crescendos and decrescendos. These exercises might look something like the ones in **FIGURES 9-1, 9-2, 9-3,** and **9-4**.

There are many more exercises of this type that you can devise to practice the heel-tap technique. Feel free to come up with your own.

In a performance situation, you will use the heel-tap technique when playing from soft to medium-loud. You will, however, find that you cannot play extremely loud with this method. The heel-tap is great for playing "four on the floor" in jazz (which you will learn about in Chapter 12) and for playing other motorlike patterns such as the bass drum rhythm to the Brazilian samba (Chapter 13). This technique can also accommodate slow to fast speeds. Lastly, the heel-tap method gets a rounded, softer tone.

If you're playing music that requires very loud, punchy bass drum

FIGURE 9-3   Bass drum exercise

FIGURE 9-4   Bass drum exercise

kicks, you must lift your entire foot and leg, then drop it on the pedal. Let's call this method the "leg-drop" technique.

The weight of your foot and leg naturally allow you to play louder when you use this method. Be certain to allow the beater to spring back after you strike the drum and always keep the bottom of your foot in contact with the footboard.

It's important to know when to use the leg-drop technique. It cannot accommodate real fast or soft rhythms. You will be able to use this technique only for loud quarter and eighth notes. It comes in handy when playing dance, rock, or pop music. However, some drummers attempt to use this technique when they play softly. Drummers who are used to playing heavy rock music tend to mistakenly use this technique when they are asked to play softly. You can tell a drummer is doing this when you hear abnormally thunderous accents amidst a backdrop of quiet music. Also, if you look at a drummer when he or she is attempting to use this technique for a soft dynamic, you will notice that they have shaky balance. Often their time suffers, too.

The Toe Technique

The next bass drum technique is used for fast, multiple, unaccented notes. It works well when playing a series of medium-loud to very loud eighth or sixteenth notes. We'll call this the "toe" technique since your ankle is not used and there is no weighty leg drop.

When you use the toe technique, you will bounce the ball of your foot and toes on the pedal. Again, allow the beater to spring back after each note.

The toe technique has its widest application in double bass drum or double pedal bass drumming. Often drummers use a double pedal or two bass drums to create rolls with their feet. The toe technique is used to do this because, more than any other method, it allows for superquick flurries of notes.

Single bass drum players use the toe technique for beats that require a long string of eighth or sixteenth notes or for combinations between the hands and the bass drum foot. Usually, these combinations mean that one or more notes are played by the hands, followed by a single bass drum note. A good example of this would be playing sixteenth notes between the right hand and the bass drum in an alternating fashion.

The Foot-Slide

The fourth and final technique uses a sliding motion. We'll call this the "foot-slide" approach. It has two parts.

The foot-slide technique is used to create very fast, loud double-stroke patterns in the bass drum. Usually they occur in various combinations with the hands. In order to use this method, you must lift your ankle and rest the ball of your foot on the pedal about a quarter to halfway up the footboard toward you. This is a start position. Once you're in this position, tap your toe on the pedal, then slide your foot onto the pedal until your entire foot rests on it. The result is really a combination of the toe technique and the leg-drop technique. To do this again, you must lift your leg and slide your toe back to the start position. When played in context, you get a sliding effect.

As stated previously, the foot-slide technique is used to create two notes in rapid succession. The first note is created by a toe tap; the second is created by the impact of the foot and the weight of the leg as it slides onto the footboard. Because of this, you may, at first, get an accent on the second note. As you practice this technique, though, you will find that, with a little work, you can even out the sound.

Some drummers think that when they play, they should wear a sneaker with a nonskid rubber sole. If you wear a shoe like this, you will have a difficult time pulling off the foot-slide technique. If you want to use this technique efficiently, you should wear a shoe with a smooth-surfaced leather or plastic sole.

Playing the Hi-Hat with Your Hands and Feet

The hi-hat consists of two medium-sized (usually 13" or 14" diameter) cymbals suspended on a stand about 1" apart. The bottom cymbal sits upside down on the stand, and the top cymbal is clamped to a thin rod that rises from inside the center of the stand's frame. A pedal, similar in size and shape to the bass drum pedal, is found at the base of the stand. The hi-hat pedal does not, however, contain a beater. When you press down on the pedal, the two hi-hat cymbals will strike one another. (See Chapter 1 for a picture of the hi-hat.)

Where to Put the Hi-Hat

If you set up the drum kit in the traditional right-handed fashion, the hi-hat will be placed on your left side. If you choose to set up lefty, your hi-hat will be placed on your right side. Either way, the hi-hat should be placed next to the snare drum and raised several inches higher than the snare drum, depending on your personal taste and the type of music you are playing.

If you're playing loud music such as rock 'n' roll, you may want to raise the hi-hat as much as a half a foot above your snare drum to keep a good spread between hands. This will allow you to play both the snare and the hi-hat loudly without getting your hands tangled up. Also, this will allow you to play on the edge of the hi-hat cymbals, where you will get a louder, crunchier sound. If you're playing soft music, you may want to raise the hi-hat only a couple of inches above the snare drum so that you can easily ride on top of the top hi-hat cymbal.

The Role of the Hi-Hat

The hi-hat is used in fills, but its primary function is to ride on and to keep time. When using it to keep time, such as in jazz, you will often use your foot. When doing this, you will clamp the two cymbals together on beats two and four to create a nonsustaining *chick* sound.

Ninety-nine percent of all drummers cross their hands when they play a beat between the snare drum and the hi-hat. If you're set up right-handed, this means that you will play the hi-hat with your right hand and the snare drum with your left hand.

Hi-Hat Foot Techniques

There are three main techniques used to play the hi-hat with your foot. The first technique is the "heel-tap" method you learned for the bass drum. The second technique is the "leg-drop" technique you also learned for the bass drum. The heel-tap method is used mostly by beginners to get used to pressing down the pedal. Its drawback is that you cannot get a loud, crisp *chick* sound. Also, your time may suffer because you're not feeling each beat physically. We will talk about this more in a moment.

The leg-drop technique has limited use as well. It should only be used to create hard accents. In this case, you will crash the two hi-hat cymbals together, then immediately release them. When you do this, the sound you get is not unlike the sound a symphonic percussionist gets when he or she crashes two concert cymbals together. The only difference is that hi-hat cymbals get a weaker, softer tone because of their size. Also, because of their set proximity to one another, you cannot crash hi-hats together with as much force as an orchestral drummer would when using concert cymbals. With regard to the hi-hat, drummers call this crash an "open" sound. The *chick* sound described earlier is referred to as a "closed" sound.

The most common hi-hat foot technique used by drummers is the "heel-toe" method. When you use this approach, you will rock your foot back and forth on the pedal between your heel and toe. As previously stated, the hi-hat typically keeps time by marking beats two and four. When using the heel-toe method, you will tap your heel on the back of the pedal on beats one and three, and then tap your toe on the pedal's incline to create a *chick* sound on beats two and four. You will not hear the sound of the heel as it hits the back of the pedal when you're playing a beat.

The most important part is to develop a rocking motion between your heel and toe. This helps you to feel the quarter note pulse, and your time will become more solid. Before using the heel-toe method in a beat, you will need to get used to it by practicing it by itself. When doing this, make sure that the *chick* sound occurs only on beats two and four.

Four-Way Coordination

Four-way coordination refers to the interaction between your hands and feet. Gradually, over the next days, weeks, months, and years, you will develop independence between your limbs. In order to play beats, fills, and solos, it will be necessary for you to achieve this type of coordination. Start with the exercises in **FIGURES 9-5, 9-6,** and **9-7** to develop foot control. First try using the heel-tap technique in the hi-hat, then try the much harder heel-toe rocking motion.

Now let's add the hands. In the first measure of **FIGURE 9-9**, you will play on the ride cymbal or hi-hat with the right hand while you play the bass drum with your right foot. In the second measure of **FIGURE 9-9**, you

FIGURE 9-5 Bass drum and hi-hat exercise

FIGURE 9-6 Bass drum and hi-hat exercise

FIGURE 9-7 Bass drum and hi-hat exercise

FIGURE 9-8 Beginning coordination exercise

FIGURE 9-9 Beginning coordination exercise

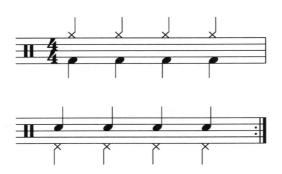

FIGURE 9-10   Basic drum set beat

FIGURE 9-11   Basic drum set beat

will use your left hand to strike the snare drum and your left foot to "click" the hi-hat.

In **FIGURES 9-10** and **9-11**, place your right hand on your ride cymbal and your left hand on the snare drum. These are basic rock beats.

Practicing Without a Drum Set

For some of you, it may be too expensive to purchase a drum set or a pad set right now. Don't fret. You can still practice some basic drum set coordination exercises without one. For example, you can try all of the figures in this chapter without the use of a drum set. You can even get some use out of practicing the beats in Chapters 11 through 16 using the following drum set simulation. It is assumed that you do have a snare drum or pad.

Sit in a straight-backed wooden chair with no arm rests. Then set up your snare or pad directly in front of you, placing it at your navel or slightly lower. Next, place a series of books or magazines on whatever tables, chairs, or other furniture you have at your disposal. Make sure that the books are easily reachable. Imagine the setup of a drum set and try your best to simulate this. For instance, you will want to place some objects higher or lower than others. Refer to Chapter 1 for setup guidelines, then label with a piece of paper which books represent the 12" and 13" rack tom-toms, the floor tom-tom, ride and crash cymbals, and the hi-hat. In place of pedals, you may simply tap your feet on the floor.

Practicing without a drum set is not desirable. It may even be a bit of a drag. However, you will get some real use out of the drum set facsimile described here. As soon as you are able, purchase a basic set. Remember, used drums and cymbals are always a viable option. You do not need to break the bank when buying a drum kit. You do not absolutely need a crash cymbal or a 13" rack tom, either. A simple four-piece kit with bass drum, hi-hat, snare drum, floor-tom, and ride cymbal will suffice.

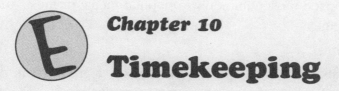

Chapter 10

Timekeeping

The single most important facet of playing the drums is time-keeping. Without a good internal clock, you will have limited ability to play with other musicians. If you want to play at a professional level, you will need to have an impeccable sense of time, because increasingly drummers are asked to play along with sequencers, samples, loops, drum machines, and other electronic media.

The Importance of Steady Playing

All music exists in time and space. Time refers to the pulse of the music, while space refers to the rhythmical components—notes and rests—that exist within a time span. Ninety-eight percent of the music that you will play on the drum set exists inside a strict box of time. This is because the drum set is used most commonly in popular music or music that has its roots in pop music.

When we talk about pop music in this book, we are not referring to the current Top 40. For our purposes, popular music includes any style of music that has earned a consistently large following and is used for entertainment (often celebratory) purposes in a public setting. In this sense, early jazz, rock 'n' roll, Latin, various ethnic musical styles, and country and western all have pop value.

Shall We Dance?

All of these genres of music have one common thread; they are all rooted in dance. Early jazz brought about the Charleston, the lindy hop, the jitterbug, and others. In the '50s, rock 'n' roll and rockabilly dancing became popular due in large part to Elvis Presley. The '60s saw the invention of the twist, but by the '70s, disco was all the rage. In the late '80s and beyond, people began free-dancing to prerecorded, electronic drum grooves. This raised the bar for real drummers who now had to compete with machines that played effortlessly and with perfect time.

Country and western music has long since been rooted in square and round dancing. Latin music is closely tied to such dances as the mambo, cha-cha, rumba, and others. Other ethnic styles of music are dance oriented as well. For example, the Irish enjoy playing and dancing to gigues and reels.

Your Role on the Bandstand

Nowadays, the drum set is called upon to propel *all* these styles of music. This is not to say that the sole purpose of the drum set is to get people out on the dance floor, but the drum set's evolution is due in large part to the development of popular dance and the demands of a public that likes to "cut a rug" to the music they see, hear, and buy.

The job of a drummer is to glue a band together, so no matter what style of music you play, you will need to focus a great deal on timekeeping. Other musicians depend on drummers for their "adhesive" qualities whether or not they like to admit it. If you ask your average bandleader what she or he is looking for in a drummer, most will probably say first and foremost, good time. To them this means more than just solid time, but the ability to smoothly guide a band through a tune by providing a comfortable springboard for a soloist and/or a singer. It is not surprising, then, when musicians complain that "the drummer rushes" or "the drummer drags," this leads to the drummer getting sacked.

If you join a band, you will be looked upon with scrutiny, and if anything goes wrong with the time or feel of the tune, the finger will most likely be pointed at you. So the question is: How do you make sure that you have solid time? Once again, the answer always comes down to practice, self-awareness, and perseverance.

Playing with Recordings

Not all of us instinctively possess a good internal clock. The good news is that you can develop excellent time by first, being aware of its importance; second, by evaluating your own playing; and, third, by doing something constructive about it. One way to develop good time is to play along with recordings.

Where to Get Recordings

These days there is an overabundance of CDs available to you. Once upon a time, the only drummers who appeared on records were quality players. Now, any Tom, Dick, or Harry can make a CD in a home studio, so you have to be careful in your selection. You want to play along with the best, not the kid next door who has rushing and/or dragging problems.

In Appendix A, you will see a list of professional drummers together with some of their most significant recordings. All of these drummers play with good time, though some of the studio players such as Vinnie Colaiuta, JR Robinson, Hal Blaine, Jeff Porcaro, Jim Keltner, Larry London, and others have a particularly acute sense of time that is worth studying.

The Studio Scene

Studio musicians most commonly dwell in Los Angeles these days, but New York City, Memphis, and Nashville can all be considered recording capitals of the world. Studio drummers typically work on a whole host of projects ranging from film and TV scores, to jingles for TV advertisements, to backing up famous singers, to standing in for a member of a rock band who has great looks, but doesn't record particularly well.

Often studio or session drummers are asked to play with a click track as they record. A click track is the same as a metronome, which you will learn about shortly. Studio drummers are constantly under the gun, because, for a music producer, time is money. Session drummers are expected to learn material quickly, play with both rhythmical clarity and accuracy, understand just about any kind of "feel" or style of music, and most of all, play with great time. So, when trying to improve your time, it's a good idea to familiarize yourself with the work of session drummers and to play along with their recordings.

Questions to Ask Yourself

When you play with recordings you will not only improve your sense of time but you will gain a sense of what it's really like to play in a band. You will also gradually learn a repertoire of tunes by playing with CDs and begin, almost through osmosis, to learn about appropriateness in drumming. Following is a list of issues to think about when playing along with recordings. Ask yourself:

- What style of music am I playing?
- What is the main groove being played by the drummer? How would you describe it?

- Where does the drummer play fills?
- Do the fills help the music to develop and climax? If so, how?
- Where does the drummer make shifts in the feel of the tune? (This may include dynamics, changing the ride pattern or ride surface, or laying out altogether in a section.)
- Is the drummer playing a lot of notes? In other words, do you detect a lot of activity or is he or she playing with a lot of space?
- What is the structure of the tune? If it's a Top 40 tune, are there verses, choruses, a bridge or middle eight, a coda?
- Is the drummer pushing the beat, laying back on the beat, or playing straight down the middle of the beat?

Playing with recordings is a simple procedure. All you need is a Discman or Walkman, a pair of headphones, and a collection of recordings to pull from. Using headphones that completely cup around your ears is a good idea, because this will minimize the sound of your drums and allow you to focus on the pulse of the recorded music. These kinds of headphones are a little more expensive, but well worth the price.

ALERT!

Be careful not to turn the music up too loud when playing along with recordings. It's better to quiet yourself down. Earphones turned up too loudly can cause hearing damage.

Metronomes

A metronome is a practice and performance aid. Basically, it's a useful timekeeping device. Metronomes are compact, plastic boxes that, create an electronic beeping sound, sometimes accompanied by a flashing light. The beeps and the lights are designed to help you maintain the pulse in music. Metronomes keep you honest about your playing. They also help you develop your internal clock.

Choosing a Metronome

There are many brands of metronomes on the market and prices range from a few bucks to well over a hundred dollars. These companies include Seiko, Wittner, Korg, Qwik Time, Yamaha, Franz, Exacto, and Boss. Some drum set manufacturers also make metronomes, such as Tama, and you can now download click tracks from the Internet. Drum machines can also serve as fancy metronomes since many of them come with a preset click track. If they don't, it's very easy to create one on any drum machine.

The best metronomes on the market are ones that can be turned up loudly and ones that come with an earphone jack. Pocket metronomes are best suited for use with softer instruments, such as violins. You need a metronome with some juice! Given this, the classic Dr. Beat DB-66 metronome and its newer counterpart, the Talking Dr. Beat DB-88 metronomes are the best on the market. The Exacto Ex-3 model is also quite good and is less expensive.

ALERT!

Whatever you use, stay far away from manual windup pendulum metronomes. These are completely obsolete now, as their time is dubious. Questionable time on a metronome defeats the purpose of even using one. In fact, it may actually hurt your playing.

The Dr. Beat DB-66 metronome offers many features such as a dual light; one light is designated for beat one, while the other light usually pulsates on the other beats in the measure. It also has multiple click sounds. You can therefore discriminate between eighth notes, sixteenth notes, or triplets. You can change the individual volume levels of these note types, too. Further, you have a wide range of tempo and meter choices, and you have a tap function. The tap function allows you to set the tempo by tapping the speed you desire.

Setting the Metronome to Meet Your Needs

There are many ways to set a metronome. If you're in 4/4, for example, you may want to set the metronome to represent all four downbeats. However, as the tempo increases, you may find it helpful to set the metronome to represent half notes. If you're having trouble playing with the metronome, you should set it so that it represents eighth notes or even sixteenth notes. Note divisions and subdivisions will help you to play with better rhythmical accuracy.

Also, don't forget to set the metronome so that the clicks and lights fit the meter or time signature you're playing. The loudest click should always represent beat one. Reading the manual that comes with your metronome is recommended so that you become aware of the full range of options your metronome has to offer.

FACT

If you set the metronome at sixty, there will be sixty clicks played per minute. Obviously, higher numbers mean more clicks per minute, while lower numbers mean less clicks per minute.

Using the Metronome as a Gauge

In Chapter 6, you learned about the step method for learning the rudiments. Using a metronome is particularly helpful when practicing this approach. The step method can be translated to meet the demands of virtually any exercise or study piece you're working on. Start by setting the metronome at a slow speed, and try playing the exercise or rudiment in question. If the tempo still feels fast, decrease the tempo.

Once you find a relaxed start tempo, practice at this speed until you feel ready to move on. At this point, increase the tempo one or two clicks, then try playing the given exercise again. Gradually increase the tempo over the period of many days or weeks and keep a written log of the tempo increases you've made.

This log will be used to evaluate your progress. Over the course of many days, you will start to see a pattern emerge. If you're making improvement, you will notice that your tempos increase at a slow but steady rate. If you're attempting to play speeds that are beyond your ability, or if you haven't found a comfortable start tempo, this will be reflected in your metronome log. In this case, you will notice that your log shows erratic tempo shifts.

> The goal is not always to play fast. Reverse the step method and see how *slowly* you can accurately play an exercise or a piece of music. You'll find that the slower you go the more space exists between notes. This makes playing slowly and in time very challenging.

Each day, you may find that you have to back up from the previous day's top speed and build from there. This is natural. Just remember not to increase the speed in large quantities or you will defeat the purpose of the step method altogether. The step method is predicated upon a gradual increase by degrees.

When using the step method, you will sooner or later come up against a wall and you will not be able to play any faster. This wall will represent your top speed on any given day. Finding your "wall" is a good thing. It allows you to set realistic and definite goals. By using the step method, together with a metronome, you will become more organized in your practice and you will be able to better monitor and evaluate your progress.

By now you should understand the importance of timekeeping and the role of drums and drummers in a group setting. Practicing with a metronome can be frustrating, so you might be tempted to turn it off during your daily workout. Don't fall into this lazy trap. Also, some students mistrust metronomes, complaining that they keep bad time. Usually, the complaint is that the metronome is dragging. Do not buy into this myth either. If you have a good metronome, it is *always* right.

The tendency with most drummers is to rush. If you get off from the metronome slightly, try to get back on without stopping. If you turn the beat around or completely lose track of the metronome's pulse, stop and count off again. It's that simple. One of the joys of the practice room is that you're allowed to make mistakes.

The metronome will emphasize many of your inadequacies. This is its job. Don't let this discourage or dishearten you. It can be exasperating playing with a click, but consistent work with a metronome will also bring about a great deal of improvement in your playing. (E)

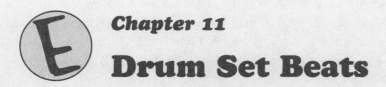

Chapter 11

Drum Set Beats

The following pages contain many basic drum set beats. The idea is to give you practical grooves that really work. In this chapter, you will learn primarily about rock 'n' roll and its derivatives, but in the process, you will also start to develop four-way coordination.

A Brief History of Rock 'n' Roll

Rock 'n' roll gained popularity in the 1950s due in large part to the development of the electric guitar, jukebox, television, and the 45 RPM record. Key figures such as Alan Freed, Sam Phillips, Jerry Leiber, Mike Stoller, and others all took advantage of this technology to draw audiences and musicians alike to participate in the birth of a new era. Like nearly all American music, rock 'n' roll grew out of the black experience, yet its most popular artist was undoubtedly Elvis Presley, who was a white kid from Tupelo, Mississippi, but sang like a black R & B singer.

The Rise of Rock 'n' Roll

Sam Phillips's record label, Sun Records, had a major impact on the rise of rock 'n' roll by signing Presley and assembling what would later be known as the Million Dollar Quartet, featuring Jerry Lee Lewis, Carl Perkins, Johnny Cash, and Presley himself.

Early rock 'n' roll contained elements of country and western, blues, gospel, R & B, and jump swing, but it soon matured into its own distinct sound and gave rise to such icons as Jimi Hendrix, the Who, the Rolling Stones, Bob Dylan, and, of course, the Beatles.

Rock was dealt a harsh blow when rap music, another black-rooted art form, topped it in CD sales in the 1990s, but it continues to thrive and have an enormous impact on popular culture. It is doubtful that rock will ever cease to be played.

Rock's Legacy

Rock 'n' roll made its crossover to white audiences when Elvis recorded "That's All Right, Mama" in 1954, though he wouldn't earn a number one hit until 1956 with "Heartbreak Hotel." In 1964, with the arrival of the Beatles on American shores, rock music firmly embedded itself into the collective consciousness of popular culture and hasn't left since.

Drums and drummers contributed greatly to the evolution of rock. In the 1960s, the rock-drumming boom occurred quite literally. This was due in part to rock's enormous popularity, which led to stadium shows and high-volume performances. Outdoor festivals hosted tens of thousands of rock enthusiasts. The Monterrey Pop Festival in 1967 drew 200,000 fans over a three-day period and Woodstock in 1969 drew some 500,000 devotees.

FACT

Rock 'n' roll has mutated into several offshoots, such as West Coast surf, garage rock, psychedelic rock, disco, progressive rock, heavy metal, punk rock, new wave, grunge, alternative rock, and other popular music styles. Many would argue that rock gave birth to techno and rap as well.

Drummers reveled in this new environment and used it as a way to be seen as well as heard. In particular, drummers such as Keith Moon (the Who), John Densmore (the Doors), Ginger Baker (Cream), Michael Shrieve (Carlos Santana), Mitch Mitchell (Jimi Hendrix), and others brought drums to the forefront by playing busier grooves and/or flashy solos.

Additionally, many of them began using larger kits that included an abundance of cymbals and double bass drums. By the mid to late '60s, drummers had cultivated rock star images of their own and often they accomplished this by including theatrics and other flashiness into their playing. The biggest exception to this was Ringo Starr, a tasty but bare-bones drummer who became a household name because he was a member of the Beatles, undoubtedly the most popular band in history.

Rockin' in the '70s

In the 1970s, rock drummers experimented more with accessories in their setups. Some went so far as to include gongs, tympani, chimes, bells, bongos, and other percussion instruments. Neil Peart (Rush) was probably the most extravagant in his setup, but others such as John Bonham (Led Zeppelin), Carl Palmer (ELP), Ian Paice (Deep Purple), and Nick Mason (Pink Floyd) experimented with augmented kits as well.

The '80s

As the 1980s dawned, a new style of drumming emerged that, oddly enough, combined Jamaican reggae with punk. This was almost single-handedly accomplished by Stewart Copeland (the Police), with Manu Katché (Peter Gabriel) to follow in 1986 with a style that borrowed from Copeland's strange but effective stylistic blend. Also in the '80s, Bill Bruford (King Crimson) and Jerry Marotta (Peter Gabriel) experimented with drum sets that did not contain any cymbals. Other drummers in this period, such as Alex Van Halen, kept increasing the size of their drum set. His boasted four bass drums!

Into the '90s and Beyond

In the early 1990s, many drummers moved to a scaled-down four-piece drum kit, hocking their splash cymbals and their double bass drums for deep tom-toms, extra-thick crash cymbals, and double bass pedals. This was influenced by the Seattle grunge movement and drummer Dave Grohl (Nirvana).

By the mid '90s, rock drummers seemed to take a backseat to electronic media as drum machines and computer-driven music dominated much of the airwaves. However, drummers responded by not only continuing to give strong performances, but by becoming adept programmers as well. Larry Mullen, Jr. (U2), Phil Selway (Radiohead), Zachary Alford (David Bowie), and others created great synthesized rhythms through the use of drum machines, and so on.

Today, drummers still have an enormous influence on rock music. Popular drummers such as Carter Beauford (Dave Matthews Band), Mike Portnoy (Dream Theater), Neil Primrose (Travis), Matt Cameron (Independent), and others continue to maintain high professional standards.

Basic Rock Grooves

Many of the basic grooves used by drummers in the mid '50s are still being used today. However, given the demands of huge venues, rock drummers generally hit much harder now. Following you will find a basic rock beat together with nine variations. These beats are very common, and on any given day, you can hear them on the radio played by your favorite bands.

Remember, the ride hand (hi-hat or cymbal) is indicated on the top space of the staff, the snare drum is indicated on the third line up from the bottom, and the bass drum is indicated on the bottom space. Also, remember that the black circular note head is not used when writing hi-hat or cymbal rhythms. Instead, an 'x' is used. This is just convention in drum set notation.

The 'x' helps to visually separate the ride hand from the snare drum, tom-toms, and bass drum. However, the 'x' does not change the rhythmical value of the note. For example, if you see an 'x' note head

 FIGURE 11-1 Basic rock beats

TRACK 36

paired up with an eighth note, it will sound exactly the same as an eighth note written with a solid black circular note head.

If you set up your kit right-handed, you will use your right hand to ride. Ride patterns are steady, repeated rhythms designed to give cohesion and, in terms of what we actually hear, high end frequency (Hz) to a beat or groove. Beats played without a ride pattern tend to sound spare or even empty; they also have less tonal color. All of the beats in this book are written with an 'x' note head in the ride hand.

Rock beats are 98 percent kick and snare. Typically, the bass drum covers notes that may occur anywhere on beats one and three, while the snare drum covers notes that occur anywhere on beats two and four. This is not an ironclad rule, though.

The following beats (**FIGURE 11-1**) utilize only eighth notes and quarter notes. You may ride on either the hi-hat or the ride cymbal when playing these beats. If you choose to ride on the cymbal, you must *chick* the hi-hat with your foot on the downbeats of two and four. When riding on the hi-hat, make sure you keep the hi-hat cymbals clamped together tightly.

Playing quarter notes on the bell of the cymbal is also common. When drummers do this, they often turn their hand in a palm-flat position so as to strike the bell of the cymbal with the shaft of the stick. Otherwise, any cymbal riding you do is best done using the thumbs-up position.

These are but a few variations on a theme. Try creating your own beats utilizing quarter note and eighth note combinations. You can also try combining these beats to create two- and four-bar phrases.

Spicing It Up

Now let's try some more advanced beats. The following grooves use sixteenth notes to spice things up. As you will see in the first beat of the first pattern, there is the familiar eighth/two sixteenths rhythm written in. The tendency will be to play the hi-hat with the bass drum on the *ah*, but you can avoid this by practicing the interaction between the hi-hat and bass drum out of tempo.

Again, looking at beat one of pattern one, you will see that the hi-hat and bass drum play together on the downbeat and the upbeat *only*. Say the following out loud when you practice this rhythm: "Together, together, bass; together, together, bass," and so on. As silly as it may seem, by saying this out loud as you practice, you will learn this pattern much more quickly. Once you learn the beats in **FIGURE 11-2**, experiment with the same ride variations you used in **FIGURE 11-1**.

The following beats (**FIGURE 11-3**) use hi-hat variations that include open and closed sounds. *Open* refers to the sound you get when you partially ease up on the hi-hat pedal as previously described. *Closed* refers to a tightly clamped-down hi-hat; this is done by using your foot

FIGURE 11-2 Intermediate rock beats

TRACK 37

to press down firmly on the pedal. The open sound is designated by an *o* written above the note. The closed sound is designated by a "+" also written above the note. If nothing is written, it is assumed that the hi-hat is played closed.

The next group of beats (**FIGURE 11-4**) use ghost notes, which create the feeling of depth in the music. A ghost note is played much softer than the other notes and is written with a parenthesis around it. Ghost notes make the music seem more relaxed and funky. Once you feel comfortable with these exercises, experiment with a quarter note ride pattern just as you did when varying **FIGURES 11-1** and **11-2**.

The final beats in this section (**FIGURE 11-5**) use sixteenth notes in the ride hand. You will now incorporate the two sixteenths/eighth pattern and the eighth/two sixteenths pattern into your playing. First, practice riding on the hi-hat. Once you gain proficiency with this, try riding on the cymbal, striking the bell of the cymbal every time you see an eighth note.

FIGURE 11-3 Open and closed hi-hat beats

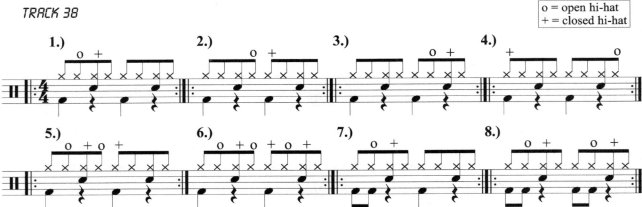

TRACK 38

FIGURE 11-4 Rock beats with ghost notes

First practice the ghost notes at an equal volume.

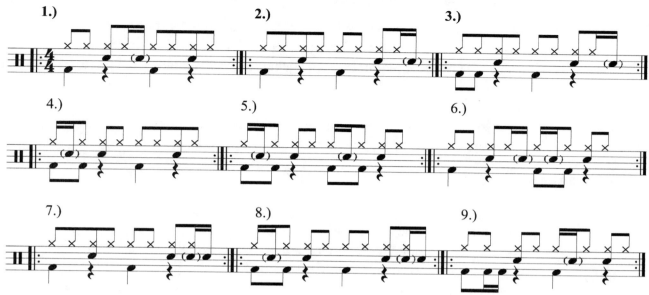

FIGURE 11-5 Using sixteenth notes in the ride hand

1 e + ah   3 e + ah

Other Popular Styles

Following you will find some basic grooves that are used in popular music. These beats will be particularly helpful to you if you find yourself working someday in a commercial setting, playing weddings, corporate functions, or various other kinds of parties and balls. These are dance rhythms that will probably always be requested at social gatherings.

If you would like to learn more about these styles, or if you would like to learn how to vary these beats, see Appendix B.

Motown

Motown is short for "Motor town" and represents a style of music that came out of the Detroit area around 1960. Motown is closely associated with Motown Records, the first black-owned record company. Motown singers were largely influenced by the blues, gospel, and R & B. This basic beat is still popular with Motown drummers. (See **FIGURE 11-6**.)

Disco

Disco gained popularity in the dance clubs of the 1970s and is still quite popular today, especially at parties and other social gatherings. (See **FIGURE 11-7**.)

Country and Western

Country and western predates rock 'n' roll but is still going strong even though there is some split between traditional country artists and crossover, or pop, country artists. Following you will find two basic country beats. A third and important beat used by country drummers is the "train rhythm," which is popular in bluegrass music. Since the train rhythm is a brushes beat, look to Chapter 17 for more information.

The country ballad uses something called a side stick. To play a side stick, turn the stick around and place it on the drumhead at about two o'clock. Rest the back of your hand on the drumhead and hold the stick using a lateral grasp. Strike the rim of the drum using a downward motion. Finding the proper spot on the stick to strike the rim is

FIGURE 11-6   Motown beat

TRACK 40

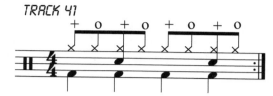

FIGURE 11-7   Disco beat

TRACK 41

FIGURE 11-8   Country ballad

TRACK 42   *Use a side stick on the snare.

FIGURE 11-9   Country swing

TRACK 43

FIGURE 11-10   Blues and gospel shuffle

TRACK 44

FIGURE 11-11   Hip-hop groove

TRACK 45 Give this beat a slight swing feel

important. There is a sweet spot about 3" or so from the butt that you'll need to find through a little trial and error. Listen to the CD to hear what **FIGURE 11-8** sounds like.

Country swing as epitomized by Texas swing uses the same triplet ride pattern found in swing music. (See **FIGURE 11-9**.) If you're unfamiliar with triplets, you may need to skip to Chapter 12 to see how they are played.

Blues and Gospel Shuffle

Blues and gospel are closely aligned musically, though the latter is a form of American devotional music. (See **FIGURE 11-10**.) These are older styles of black music that predate both rock and jazz. Again, you will see the use of triplets. For more information on this type of rhythm see Chapter 12.

Hip-Hop

Hip-hop is currently a very popular style of "street" music. It melds together many predominantly black American styles of music including funk, soul, jazz, rap, and techno. **FIGURE 11-11** shows a basic groove.

The beats written out in this chapter are really only the beginning. Because the musical genres discussed here are so popular and expansive, it's important that you familiarize yourself with a wide range of recordings from these idioms. Transcribe drum parts from these albums and make up your own exercises so that you gain greater fluency with each style. You should also review Appendices A and B for more information on rock music, its forerunners, and its offshoots.

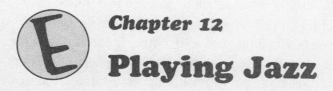

Chapter 12

Playing Jazz

In this chapter, you will learn about the history of jazz and begin to play basic jazz rhythms. You will also be confronted with triplets, a common rhythm in jazz music. Contemporary jazz requires great independence between your four limbs, so we will learn to play this style one step at a time.

A Brief History of Jazz

After the American Civil War, a new style of music began to slowly take shape. By 1895, jazz had emerged in New Orleans, Louisiana. Early jazz blended the syncopated rhythms of ragtime, the downtrodden candor of the blues, and the liveliness of New Orleans brass bands to create a fresh sound that relied more on improvisation than predetermined composition. The spontaneity of this music and the colorful nature of many of its early practitioners caused black audiences to become enamored with jazz, and it flourished in brothels and gritty drinking establishments in the American South. Soon white musicians got in on the act and formed their own jazz ensembles, though the white status quo wouldn't fully embrace jazz until the swing era of the '30s and '40s.

The Jazz Age

Jazz may have remained a regional phenomenon if it wasn't for a boom in the then infantile recording industry and a consensus among New Orleans jazzers that they take to the road to reach new audiences. Many of these musicians ended up in Chicago, where they infected audiences of all colors with this new "hot" sound.

FACT

Excluding American Indian tribal music, jazz is probably the only truly American musical style.

When a virtuoso cornet player named Louis Armstrong headed north to New York City, jazz got yet another boost. New Yorkers found Armstrong love-able and exciting, and fellow horn players found his music to be undeniably brilliant. Pretty soon, most of his contemporaries began to copy his entire approach.

By 1935, swing music captivated audiences throughout the nation due in large part to the popularity of the radio. It was during this period that drummers, and the drum set itself, began to get real notice. Still in its early stages of development, the drum set was becoming an instrument of choice with America's youth, who were inspired by stellar performances by such touring drummers as Chick Webb (Chick Webb Orchestra), Gene Krupa

(Benny Goodman Orchestra), Cozy Cole (Cab Calloway), Jo Jones (Count Basie Orchestra), and the inimitable Buddy Rich (Tommy Dorsey Orchestra).

Jazz in the '40s and '50s

By 1946, the swing era was declining rapidly, and by the mid 1950s, America's youth had swapped swing for rock 'n' roll altogether. After World War II, however, jazz continued to thrive, but it was about to undergo major changes.

In the late '40s, a new style of jazz called bebop gave birth to many of jazz's most celebrated drummers, namely, Max Roach, Kenny Clarke, and Roy Haynes. The fathers of modern jazz drumming, these players ushered in a whole new approach to playing the drum set. For example, they were among the first to develop intricate left-hand and bass drum comping techniques, as you will learn about later in the chapter.

As substyles of jazz emerged, players such as Elvin Jones, Art Blakey, Philly Joe Jones, Paul Motian, and many others added their own distinctive stamp to the music, and thus contributed to jazz's rapid percussive advances.

Contemporary Jazz

Contemporary jazz, beginning with bebop, brought about radical changes in the ways drummers interacted with a band. Bop drummers were the first to reject the idea that the drums should be used for timekeeping purposes only or for flashy, crowd-rousing cadenza solos. Also, bebop artists found themselves playing small, listening clubs, not large crowded ballrooms. Since jazz was becoming more intimate, drummers began experimenting more with subtle tone colors (especially on cymbals) and knotty rhythmic counterpoint. Further, rudimental solos became more and more passé, as the desire to create melodic lines, like that of a horn, became more prevalent.

Increasingly, drummers used space more in their playing, and they began to incorporate rhythmic phrases that were angular and disjointed. They created patterns that didn't necessarily end on downbeats or even upbeats. They left dangling sixteenth notes and other unresolved flourishes of notes. Also, they began using polymetrics to coast over bar lines. Polymetrics is the superimposing of two or more time signatures on top of one another. The rhythms that result are called polyrhythms.

Drummers such as Tony Williams (Miles Davis), Elvin Jones (John

Coltrane), and others also began using a great deal of metric modulation, which in basic terms is the morphing of one time signature into another.

In the 1960s, jazz became a vehicle for freewheeling, unbridled expression. The avant-garde jazz movement pushed the boundaries of harmony and rhythm to the very edge. In many cases, the music played had no specific time signature or even tempo, nor did it have any pre-conceived harmonic underpinning. This allowed drummers a great deal of freedom of expression, as they were able to completely separate themselves from a traditional timekeeping role.

Jazz drummers regularly experiment with a wide variety of drum setups and drumming styles. The jazz-drumming lexicon is constantly being revised as drummers reinterpret the teachings and artistry of previous generations, and as drummers become influenced by other cultures, styles of music, and advances in technology.

Other jazz players in the '60s and '70s began to explore genre combinations such as Brazilian jazz, Afro-Cuban jazz, and rock-jazz. By the '80s and '90s, some artists were even merging jazz with rap or techno. These changes forced jazz drummers to become more versatile, or multifaceted.

Since the decline of the swing era, jazz has never lost its ponderous, intellectual foundation as evidenced by its complex use of melody, harmony, and rhythm. On the other hand, jazz has also managed to maintain its roots in the blues and in popular song. More than anything, jazz continues to be a creative, improvisatory art form.

Using Triplets

Perhaps the most important rhythm used in jazz is the triplet. So far, the rhythms you've learned have all been duple patterns, which are divisible by two. A triplet, on the other hand, contains three parts. You should gradually familiarize yourself with half note triplets, quarter note triplets, eighth note triplets, and sixteenth note triplets, or sextuplets. In this chapter, we will focus primarily on the eighth note triplet.

FIGURE 12-1   Triplet exercise

RLRLRLRLRLRL   RLRLRLRLRLRL   RLRLRLRLRLRL   RLRLRLRLRLRL

FIGURE 12-2   Triplet exercise

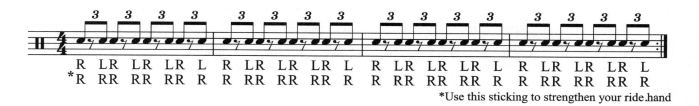

R LR LR LR L R LR LR LR L R LR LR LR L R LR LR LR L
*R RR RR RR R R RR RR RR R R RR RR RR R R RR RR RR R

*Use this sticking to strengthen your ride hand

You can count eighth note triplets many ways, but it is recommended that you count using "one-trip-let, two-trip-let, three-trip-let, four-trip-let," and so on. Before you try the eighth note triplet exercise in **FIGURE 12-1**, listen to the CD for assistance.

Once you feel comfortable with the previous exercise, try taking out the middle triplet note. By doing this, you will have a shuffle pattern. Play the exercise in **FIGURE 12-2** on your snare drum first in an alternating fashion. Then, play the pattern on your ride cymbal using just your ride hand.

Basic Ride Pattern

Unlike rock, the ride cymbal and the hi-hat foot are the most important elements in a swing beat. The most common jazz ride pattern looks like **FIGURE 12-3**.

You will notice that accents occur on all four downbeats, with beats one and three written in parenthesis. Tempo affects the accents that you

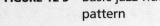

FIGURE 12-3 Basic jazz ride pattern

FIGURE 12-4 Up-tempo jazz ride pattern

TRACK 46

TRACK 47

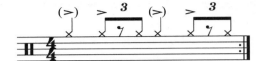

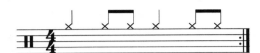

will play. If you're playing slowly, include all four accents. As you increase the speed, you will lessen the accents on beats one and three. At fast speeds, you will omit the accents on one and three altogether. At ultrafast speeds, the pattern straightens out to look like **FIGURE 12-4**.

Four-Beat and Two-Beat Feels

4/4 jazz breaks down into two basic feels: a two-beat feel and a four-beat feel. Your ability to connect rhythmically with the bass player is very important when playing these grooves. You will want to play the four-beat feel when you hear the bass player "walking." To walk on the bass means to play a driving quarter note pattern.

Since the bass player will be playing on all four beats per measure, you'll want to emulate this with your bass drum. You'll also want to dig into the cymbal more when playing a four-beat feel. When playing a four-beat bass drum feel, do not pound out the quarter notes with your foot. That is one way to ruin the swing. Instead, feather the drum softly; the quarter notes should be more felt than heard.

FIGURE 12-5 shows some examples of four-beat patterns. The first one is the basic groove, while the other two are common variations. In the variations, you'll notice that triplets have been omitted on certain beats. This is done to emphasize the quarter note pulse.

The two-beat feel is used when the bass player plays quarter notes *only* on beats one and three. In **FIGURE 12-6** you'll see the two most common two-beat patterns.

FIGURE 12-5   Four-beat patterns

TRACK 48

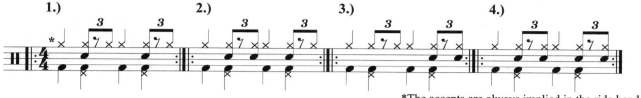

*The accents are always implied in the ride hand.

FIGURE 12-6   Two-beat patterns

TRACK 49

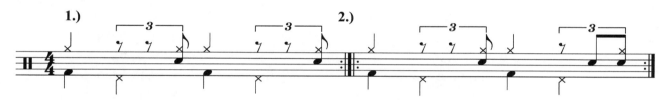

FIGURE 12-7   Jazz patterns with side stick and tom-toms

You'll notice that there is no snare drum written in these beats, with the exception of the second two-beat pattern. For all of the other grooves, you may add the snare on the downbeats of two and four. In a real situation, this may be warranted on occasion, but playing a backbeat on the snare drum can also be quite hokey, especially if you're playing modern jazz. A hipper way to do this is to use a side stick (see Chapter 11) on downbeats two and four. Better still is using a side stick on beat four only. Side stick patterns are common in jazz, and there are many at your disposal. Listen for them on recordings.

One typical side stick pattern also utilizes the rack tom on beat two. This tom-tom/rim combination is a simulation of a common conga drum pattern. (See **FIGURE 12-7**.)

FIGURE 12-8 Jazz waltz

TRACK 50

Waltz Time

We have not discussed 3/4 time yet in this book. A 3/4 time signature means that there are three beats in a measure and the quarter note gets, or receives, one beat. This means that 3/4 is identical to 4/4 except that now one full beat has been sliced off the end of the measure.

3/4 is also called waltz time and has been used in classical music for centuries. It first appeared in dance music in the eighteenth century, but the most famous waltzes were written by the nineteenth-century Viennese composers Joseph Lanner and Johann Strauss, Sr., and Johann Strauss, Jr.

3/4 often has a dainty feel and it has been used effectively in jazz for many years now. One of the great jazz waltz composers was pianist Bill Evans, who used it quite naturally in several of his pieces for jazz trio. **FIGURE 12-8** shows some basic jazz waltz patterns.

Comping on the Snare Drum

Comping was standardized in jazz drumming during the bebop era. The basic idea is to maintain a steady beat using the ride cymbal, bass drum, and hi-hat, while the snare drum hand plays or jabs syncopated patterns into the music at will. If the drummer is good, these patterns are not random, but rather, the result of interplay between the drummer and a soloist.

Comping is not easy and requires a lot of patience when practicing. However, if you learn how to comp well, you will be well on your way toward gaining four-way coordination. When playing the following

FIGURE 12-9 Snare drum comping

TRACK 51

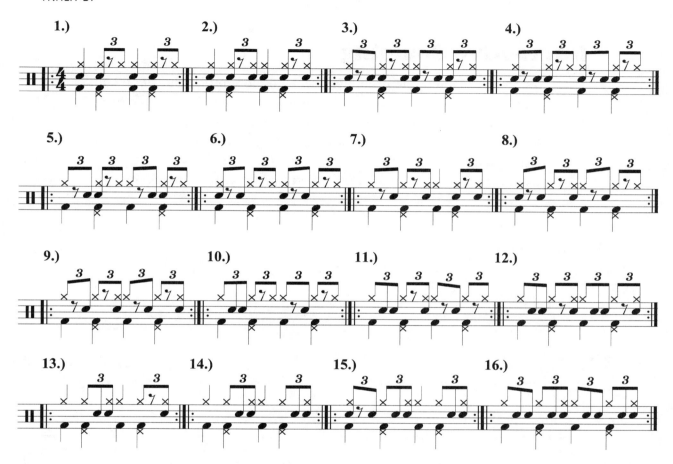

exercises, observe how the rhythms are vertically aligned. Notes that are stacked on top of each other sound at the same time. It's a good idea to practice only the ride and snare at first. Once you feel comfortable with this, add the feet. Make sure you always maintain a good triplet feel throughout. This is how you will make these patterns really swing.

The examples in **FIGURE 12-9** are but a few of the permutations available to you. Try making up your own exercises or transcribing patterns from bebop recordings. You may also combine these exercises to make up two- and four-bar phrases.

Interactive Comping

As bebop matured and drummers became more proficient with their hands and feet, many of them began experimenting with interactive comping. At first, this included playing patterns between the snare hand and the bass drum, but soon drummers began freeing up the hi-hat so that it did not always *chick* on beats two and four. This placed more emphasis on the ride hand to sustain the groove, but altering the hi-hat

FIGURE 12-10 Interactive comping

TRACK 52

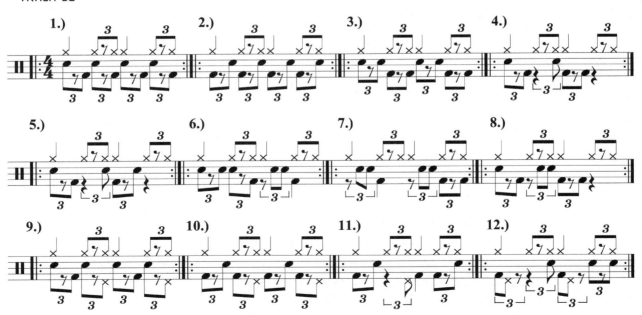

*For ease in reading, the hi-hat has been omitted from 1-8. However, make sure you play it on 2 and 4.

FIGURE 12-11   Jazz ride variations

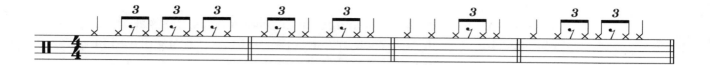

also added great color and nuance to the music, so the tradeoff was well worth it.

Interactive comping can be very difficult and we're taking a big leap from ordinary snare drum comping to these advanced four-way coordination patterns. However, with careful practice, you can learn how to play these beats. You will need to practice the beats in **FIGURE 12-10** very slowly at first and, no matter what, do not lose the triplet feel or allow your time to suffer.

These are but a few examples of interactive comping. Once you learn these patterns, come up with your own exercises or transcribe patterns from contemporary jazz CDs.

Finally, there are a number of ride variations that can be used on two- and four-beat feels. The following examples are but three choices. Whatever you use, don't stray too far from the basic ride pattern in a performance situation. Use these patterns only to add variety to the music. To get used to them, try replacing the ride pattern used in **FIGURES 12-9** and **12-10** with the three patterns shown in **FIGURE 12-11**.

Developing an Ear for Jazz

Learning any style of music requires listening to a great deal of recordings. You cannot just read about music to learn how to play it. You must immerse yourself in a particular musical culture and listen to the music to really understand it.

The best way to develop an ear for jazz is to go out and hear professional groups play live. Also, check out as many jazz recordings as you can get your hands on. Rock and Top 40 will probably come to you more naturally, even if you are not a fan of these styles of music. This is because you're surrounded by them almost everywhere you go; you are conditioned to it.

If you go to a shopping mall, restaurant, supermarket, gas station, etc., chances are you will hear rock or current chart toppers being played in the background. You may not realize it, but these styles pervade your subconscious each and every day. They're played on television, in movies, and in a variety of public places; this is not to mention on most radio stations.

Jazz, however, may pose more of a problem for you especially if you haven't heard much of it. It's not just the notes you play, it is the interpretation of those notes that counts, so listen, listen, listen. This is the best way to get acquainted with any kind of music. Ⓔ

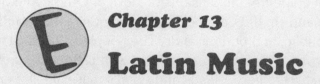

Chapter 13

Latin Music

In this chapter, you will learn some of the basic drum set grooves used in Latin music. This includes many rhythms from Brazil, Argentina, Cuba, Trinidad, and Jamaica. The purpose of this chapter is to acquaint you with some common ethnic styles of music, and to give you a needed historical perspective on each style.

A Brief History of Latin Music

Latin is a group of musical styles. It includes such a wide range of genres that it would be impossible to summarize its history in this book without giving short shrift to many of its critical movements and chief innovators. Suffice to say, "Latin" is the pat term used to mean a whole array of musical idioms that come from inhabitants of Mexico, Central and South America and the islands in the Caribbean, including Cuba, Puerto Rico, the Dominican Republic, and other islands. The people of Jamaica and Trinidad and Tobago also play music associated with Latin, but significant differences occur between these islands and Cuba's musical followers.

Varieties of Latin

While Latin music differs greatly depending on the region and country, it all has its roots in Africa, namely the musical cultures of Nigeria, Angola, and the Congo. As well, European folk music, especially Spanish music, influenced early Latin styles. Most recently, American jazz and rock has had a definite impact on Latin's evolution.

FACT

Latin music revolves around themes of love, romance, and social and political injustices. It is marked by dances, and is used for the purposes of celebration, spiritual enhancement, and cultural preservation.

The drum kit has been applied only in twentieth-century Latin music and we can break its use down into three main categories: Latin jazz, Latin pop, and other Island music. Latin jazz dates back to the early 1900s. For example, the Argentinean tango was used in a section of W. C. Handy's now classic tune "St. Louis Blues." During the '30s, Duke Ellington, influenced by valve trombonist Juan Tizol, wrote the now-famous "Caravan" and other Latin-flavored pieces.

The Latin Explosion

After World War II, the Latin jazz explosion occurred, due in part to Dizzy Gillespie, a bebop trumpeter who came under the spell of Cuban music. By the 1950s, Latin bands led by Tito Puente, Chico O'Farrill, Perez Prado, and Machito sparked many of the trends in dance that we now consider standard fare; these include the cha-cha and the mambo. The charming Desi Arnaz also helped to broaden Latin's appeal through performances by his orchestra on the hit television show *I Love Lucy*.

Over the last several decades, many virtuosic performers have emerged in Afro-Cuban music, including alto saxophonist Paquito D'Rivera, trumpeter Arturo Sandoval, pianist Michel Camillo, and others. Drum set players Steve Gadd, Alex Acuña, Don Alias, Robert Ameen, Paulo Braga, Antonio Sanchez, and Horacio "El Negro" Hernandez have also added greatly to the appeal and development of this style by studying and building upon each style's African roots and inventing clever drum set beats that simulate well the sounds of Latin percussion instruments.

Afro-Cuban drum set players imitate the sounds of instruments such as congas, claves, guiros, and timbales. A good Latin drum set player can sound like two or more hand percussionists at once, since they use a variety of pedals and accessories to layer each groove. Often these drummers use ostinatos, or repeated rhythmic patterns, to generate a fine weave of musical textures that are quite expressive—and quite impressive to listen to!

The Bossa Nova

In the '60s, the bossa nova emerged in Brazil. Its most important composer, Antonio Carlos Jobim, combined relaxed samba rhythms with cool jazz. He found the perfect blend in tunes such as "Desafinado" and "One Note Samba." Both became hits in the United States.

Just as some began to write the bossa nova off as a passing fad, guitarist/singer João Gilberto teamed up in 1963 with saxophonist Stan Getz and Jobim to record an album entitled simply Getz/Gilberto. The last-minute addition of João's then-wife, Astrud, on vocals on a tune called "The Girl from Ipanema" proved to be quite eventful. "Ipanema" became not only a megahit, but it was canonized in the history of popular music. Today, the bossa nova and its innovators are now closely associated with Brazilian culture. In fact, the government even named the airport in Rio de Janeiro after Jobim.

Latin's Influence on Other Music Forms

Latin pop has a wide fan base as evidenced by rock musicians Carlos Santana and David Byrne, and pop singers Gloria Estefan, Jon Secada, Ricky Martin, Jennifer Lopez, and Julio and Enrique Iglesias, who are father and son. Drummers Walfredo Reyes, Jr., and others have maintained strong Afro-Cuban components in Latin pop, despite the otherwise commercialization of this style by record labels.

Modern incarnations of merengue, which rarely use the drum set, are very popular with young Latinos today. Its lively feel, marked by thumping quarter notes, has proved infectious in discotheques across North America. Like most Latin styles, however, the meringue's history goes all the way back to the slave trade.

The island of Trinidad, where the steel drum was popularized, and Jamaica, where reggae was conceived, also regularly use the drum set. In Trinidad, the drum set is used mostly to accompany steel drum or pan players. Usually, a drummer will play along with steel bands in competitions or on the streets and beachfronts at dance gatherings.

The colloquial music of Trinidad is written mostly in major keys, and has a carefree lilting feel. Styles include calypso, soca, and other subgenres such as rapso and zouk, the latter being a style popular with Creole and French-speaking inhabitants of the West Indies. Like the merengue, drum set players typically emphasize the quarter note pulse in the bass drum when playing socas and rapsos. This gives the music its forward momentum and its ultramodern dance appeal.

The Emergence of Reggae and Ska

Jamaican reggae bands, at first blush, look similar to rock groups, as they often use guitars, keyboards, and electric bass. Usually there is also a front man or lead singer. The most famous crossover reggae singer is probably the late, great Bob Marley. He claimed that the word *reggae* was really borrowed from the Spanish and that it meant "the king's music."

Reggae is a bouncy style of Caribbean music that borrows from African rhythms, the blues, American pop, and most recently, rap music. But unlike rock, it stresses the upbeats, or *ands*, and often a loose triplet feel. Quarter note triplets are popular with drummers when filling, and drummers almost never use a ride cymbal in this music. In general, reggae is very hi-hat and side stick oriented. You could also say that reggae has a kind of swing to it. Very few other Latin styles contain this feature.

FACT

The etymology of the word *reggae* is arguable. Some say that it was formally used first by Toots and the Maytals on a 1968 single called "Do the Reggae," but others trace its origins back much further. The music itself is very old. Proto versions of reggae date all the way back to a tribe called the Regga who lived in West Africa.

Over the last thirty-odd years, reggae has been widely used by non-Jamaicans in pop settings. For example, Paul Simon used a reggae feel for his 1972 hit, "Mother and Child Reunion," heard on his first self-titled solo outing. Also, the jazzy pop singer Sting used a reggae groove in his tune "Love Is the Seventh Wave," on his 1985 release *Dream of the Blue Turtles*. Further, the eclectic singer Bobby McFerrin scored a big hit with his reggae-inflected tune "Don't Worry, Be Happy," from his 1988 release *Simple Pleasures*. Finally, blues and pop singer Bonnie Raitt experimented with a combination of reggae and country rock on her 1989 hit "Have a Heart," from the album *Nick of Time*.

Ska music is a close relative to reggae and it has been in existence since roughly the early 1960s. Ska has undergone many changes throughout the decades. Ska's most recent incarnations have been marked by very fast tempos and high-octane performances. Like reggae, the after-beat, or "and," is always stressed in this music and many of the biggest proponents in ska's second wave were actually British bands such as the Beat, the Specials, Madness, and others. Often elements of punk rock were combined with ska to infuse the music with a kind of "rude boy" attitude. The American ska group the Mighty Mighty Bosstones remains quite popular today.

Drums in Latin Music

Unlike jazz, Latin drummers don't necessarily use syncopation to offset or interrupt the pulse of the music; Latin is naturally syncopated. It does not contain sudden or unexpected rhythmical jabs like jazz does. Instead, syncopations are built into the music; they are fundamental to the very structure of each groove.

Afro-Cuban drummers, for instance, probably don't think about four beats with sixteenth note subdivisions when they play. If anything, they think of sixteen equal beats. Similarly, they probably don't think of four beats that divide into twelve neatly spaced eighth note triplets. If anything, they think of twelve equal beats. This gives the music great rhythmical equality.

While beats are generally felt equally, the ubiquitous clave pattern epitomizes Latin's propensity toward unequal bar divisions. As you will soon learn, the clave pattern is based on a 3+2 or a 2+3 pulsation. By doing this, this rhythm floats over downbeats, creating a hypnotic polymetric feel.

Phasing is also an important part of Latin music. Latin's divisional underpinning allows complex syncopations to sound quite smooth and organic because its practitioners do not necessarily think in short blocks of time such as two- or four-beat measures. Rather, they concern themselves with longer strings of notes that do not necessarily fall into perfectly wrapped boxes of time.

Finally, the 1:2 ratio found in European notation does not always apply well to Latin styles. You *can* notate Latin music in order to get a basic idea of how to interpret the rhythms. However, in order to make each groove breathe properly, you need to listen to the music itself.

These general descriptions of Latin styles are more a way to categorize this music rather than to shed in-depth light on each culture. Certainly, as musical styles fan out and combine with other genres, strict categorizing becomes quite difficult if not altogether impossible.

Musicians themselves use narrower terms to describe the type of Latin music they play. For instance, in Cuba alone, musicians will discriminate between salsa—a generic term for Afro-Cuban music—based in Havana and salsa found in the countryside. The important thing to remember is that Latin music has many subgenres, just as do rock and jazz. Furthermore, it is continually evolving and changing.

Brazilian Music

The samba, bossa nova, and baião are all key Brazilian styles. Like all other Latin musical styles, their roots lie in the African slave trade. The ancestral background of Brazilian music can be traced back to the Bantu or Angolan slaves who were brought to Brazil in the seventeenth, eighteenth, and nineteenth centuries.

The Samba

The samba is the centerpiece of Brazilian musical culture and originated from Bahia (now Salvador), in northeastern Brazil. There are many subgenres of samba that have been popularized over the years, and samba schools now exist where young people go to learn about this great Brazilian tradition.

Sambas are traditionally played by large groups of drummers as they march down the street in parade fashion. It is also played in drum circles. In either case, the drummers usually accompany a soloist, which may be a singer or a group of singers.

For our purposes, we'll focus on the jazz samba. To play this type of samba, you must first learn the basic foot pattern. (See **FIGURE 13-1**.) Notice the accent on beat three. The bass drum mimics the large drum called a *surdo,* which is played with a mallet in traditional settings.

The next step is learning the basic 2+3 clave pattern. (See **FIGURE 13-2**.)

FIGURE 13-1   Samba foot pattern

FIGURE 13-2   2+3 clave pattern

FIGURE 13-3 Basic jazz samba

TRACK 53

FIGURE 13-4 Samba variation

Now, let's try a basic samba pattern. (See **FIGURE 13-3**.)

Finally, let's try a more complex samba groove. There are many variations that you can use when playing the samba. (See **FIGURE 13-4**.)

Come up with your own variations, too!

Bossa Nova

As previously mentioned, the bossa nova combines traditional Brazilian rhythms with cool jazz. The bossa nova is not as festive or energetic as the samba. True bossa novas are atmospheric and tranquil. Above all else, they are quite romantic. Do not pound out these beats. Be gentle in your approach.

In order to play the bossa nova, you need to know the 3+2 clave pattern. You will play this as a side stick on your snare drum. By the way, this same clave pattern is used all the time in Cuban music, too. It is shown in **FIGURE 13-5**.

You'll notice that there are three notes played in the first measure and two notes played in the second measure, thus we get a 3+2 revolving pattern. It's hipper to alter the second measure so that you play on the *and* of three. This variation is shown in **FIGURE 13-6**.

Let's add the ride cymbal in eighth notes to complete the bossa nova feel. You may also place a brush in your ride hand and play the eighth notes on the snare drum. (See **FIGURE 13-7**.)

Now let's reverse the clave pattern so that we have a 2+3 feel. (See **FIGURE 13-8**.)

FIGURE 13-5   3+2 clave pattern

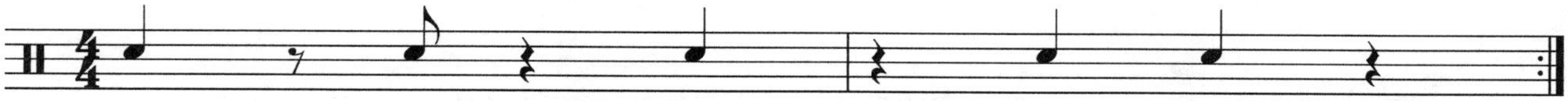

FIGURE 13-6   3+2 clave variation

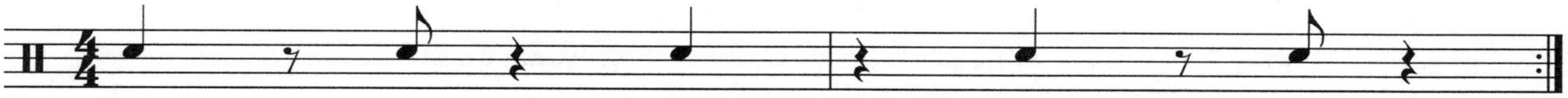

FIGURE 13-7   Basic bossa nova

TRACK 54

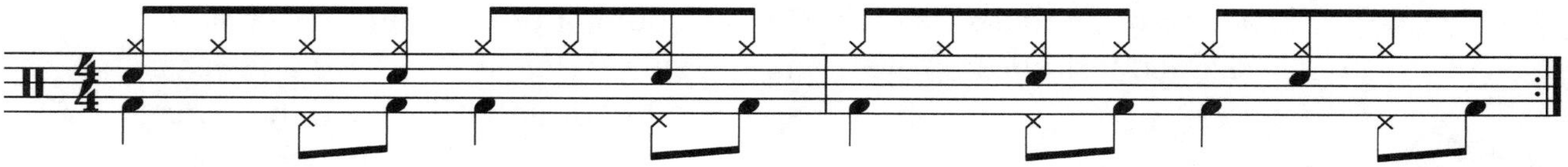

FIGURE 13-8   2+3 clave bossa nova

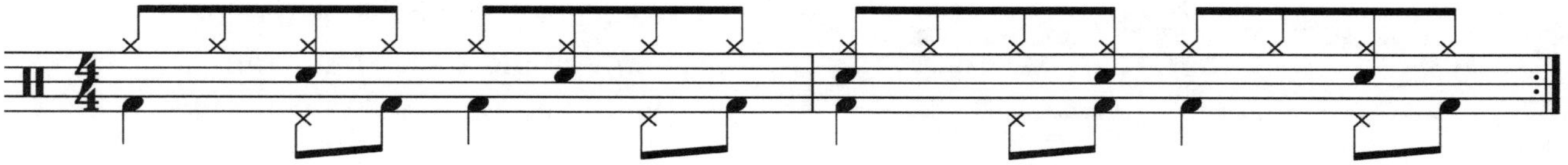

FIGURE 13-9 Bossa nova variations

TRACK 55

Finally, let's try a couple of clave, or side stick, variations. (See **FIGURE 13-9**.)

Baião

The baião is a type of dance developed in Ceará, a northeastern state in Brazil. Today, its popularity has extended to other regions and curious drum set players have come up with an adaptation that can be used in a variety of settings.

Traditionally, the baião is played on a zabumba drum, which is a double-skinned instrument played on both sides. One side creates a lower, bass drum effect while the other side creates higher-pitched notes.

In the pattern shown in **FIGURE 13-10**, the bass drum simulates the lower pitches of the zabumba and the hands simulate the higher pitches. Play the left hand on the snare drum and the right hand on a bell of your ride

FIGURE 13-10 Baião

TRACK 56

cymbal or the rim of your floor tom. You can also experiment with a "snares off" sound.

Learn the hands and feet separately then gradually put them together. You will notice that the hi-hat foot *chicks* on all four downbeats. The right hand plays with the bass drum and the left hand fills in the holes on the snare. As with all of the figures in this chapter, **FIGURE 13-10** is but one groove option. There are lots of variations or alterations drummers use.

Afro-Cuban Grooves

The following beats are common Afro-Cuban patterns that work well on the drum set. They are derived from various regions in Cuba and surrounding islands such as Puerto Rico and the Dominican Republic.

Afro-Cuban music is the result of influences from Mexico, Venezuela, Colombia, and Europe, namely the music of Spain. Indigenous, or Native American, music influenced early Cuban styles as well.

The three basic styles of Cuban music are danzón, son, and rumba. For our purposes, we'll concentrate on the rumba and its offshoots as it has interacted with the drum set on American shores in cities such as Miami and New York.

Rumba

The rumba is considered by many to be the heartbeat of Cuban music, as it gave rise to the mambo, bolero, cha-cha, and other significant dance styles. The rumba has three distinct styles: the guaguancó, columbia, and yambú. The guaguancó is probably the most widely played in Cuba's capital city of Havana.

After World War I, the term *rumba* was the generic term used by Americans to describe a variety of imported Cuban dances. Some of these styles included the pregón, the canción, and the bolero. By the '40s and '50s, society bands in New York City and elsewhere freely interpreted this music, giving rise to watered-down versions of the aforementioned styles. Thus, the American rumba was born.

FIGURE 13-11 shows two Americanized rumbas. You can use either the hi-hat or the bell of a ride cymbal on the first beat. The second beat utilizes only drums. With both beats, be sure to turn off your snares, in order to imitate the sound of conga drums more accurately.

Mambo

The first person to market the mambo was Perez Prado, who introduced it to dancers in Havana, Cuba, in 1943. The mambo fuses big band jazz and Cuban music together to create a fiery style of music that became all the rage in New York and Miami in the '40s. Because of the ferocious nature of the dancing, the mambo was called "diabolo" or "the devil's dance" by some of its detractors.

Like the rumba, the mambo's origins can be traced back to an exchange between Europe and Africa through the slave trade. Many believe that Haitians living in settlements in Cuba had a large role in its final emergence.

When playing the basic beat shown here in **FIGURE 13-12**, make sure you ride on the bell of your cymbal and use a side stick on the snare

FIGURE 13-11 Rumba patterns

TRACK 57

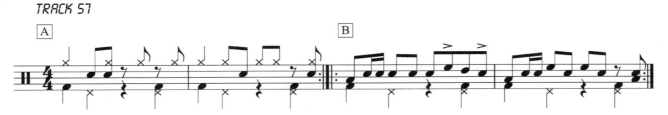

FIGURE 13-12 Mambo

TRACK 58

drum. The side stick together with the indicated tom-tom rhythm mimics the sound of conga drums.

Cha-Cha

FIGURE 13-13 Cha-cha

TRACK 59

The cha-cha is related to the mambo but it is generally slower and, these days, often more refined. It grew in popularity in dance halls in the 1950s. Cuban violinist Enrique Jorrin is credited with naming it after he heard a distinct scraping sound coming from the feet of mambo dancers. **FIGURE 13-13** is a basic cha-cha.

Bembe

Bembe is a Cuban style of music that evolved from the ritualistic rhythms of the Yoruba, a people of southwest Nigeria. The word itself is used to describe not only a musical style, but the actual drum that is used. The drum is usually double-sided and made of mango, avocado, or almaciga wood together with an animal skin. The word *bembe* is also used to describe the various ceremonies in which this music is performed. (See **FIGURE 13-14**.)

American drum set players have devised a simulation of this groove that is written in 6/8 time. 6/8 means that there are six beats in a measure while the eighth note gets one beat. Usually, 6/8 is felt in two. You will learn more about 6/8 and other time signatures in Chapter 16.

FIGURE 13-14 Bembe

TRACK 60

*Use a side stick on the snare.

Songo

Songo combines elements from the rumba, son, and other contemporary non-Latin styles, such as jazz and funk. Many contend that the contemporary artist, Juan Formell and his band Los Van Van were the first to bring this Cuban subgenre to the fore, but the songo is really probably the result of decades of experimentation.

Because this style is relatively new, the drum set has a definitive place within it. Following are a couple of songo patterns, but, first, you need to learn the basic foot pattern called the tumbao, shown in **FIGURE 13-15**.

Now, let's build on top of this ostinato using your hands. Like other beats in this chapter, learn the hands and feet individually, then gradually put them together. You'll notice that the sticking gets quite complex with songo patterns. (See **FIGURE 13-16**.)

FIGURE 13-15 Tumbao foot pattern

FIGURE 13-16 Songo

TRACK 61

A Use bell of cymbal and side stick.

B Use bell of cymbal and snare

For a simpler version of this groove, try this rock songo pattern (**FIGURE 13-17**). You'll hear Latin rock artists like Carlos Santana using this groove a lot in their music. Notice how you strike the snare drum with your left hand on the *and* of beat four. When doing this, swing your left hand under your right hand. Play at a fast tempo!

Mozambique

Mozambique is attributed to Pedro Izquierdo, a.k.a. Pello el Afrokán, but like all Latin grooves, the Mozambique borrows from a myriad of dance styles that go way back in history. This beat (**FIGURE 13-18**) is quite tricky, as you ride both on the body and the bell of your cymbal. Again, be sure to learn the hands and feet separately before attempting to put them together.

FIGURE 13-17   Rock songo

FIGURE 13-18   Mozambique

TRACK 62

Argentinean Tango

The most significant style of music to come out of Argentina is the tango. The origins of the tango are nebulous. However, it is generally believed that the tango borrowed from the Afro-Uruguayan rhythm called the candombe and other various rhythms found throughout the Argentinean flatlands.

Like nearly all Latin music, the tango is traditionally played sans drum set. However, society bands that play this style in ballrooms across the United States require the drum set player to mimic the sounds of the bandoneon, which is the most prevalent instrument used in this style. (The great tango composer Astor Piazzolla played this accordion-like instrument.)

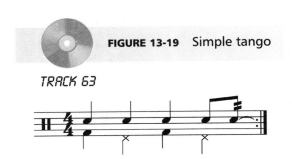

FIGURE 13-19 Simple tango

TRACK 63

The Americanized version of the tango stresses the music's marchlike qualities and its sultry appeal. The basic beat used by drum set players is quite simple. (See **FIGURE 13-19**.) Keep your snares on for this one.

Other Island Music

Other important music to come out of the Caribbean Islands includes the music of Trinidad and the music of Jamaica. As previously stated, these islands have a distinct approach to music that differs quite a bit from Cuba and its musical followers.

Calypso

Calypso is the result of multicolonialism. Slaves were originally brought over from Africa by the Spanish to work on sugar plantations in Trinidad. Later, an influx of French-speaking people influenced the patois dialect, which was used to sing this music.

In 1956, Harry Belafonte recorded a calypso album that featured the tune "Banana Boat Song," which soon became an international hit. His album entitled simply *Calypso* sold over a million copies and introduced calypso to the world stage.

British colonialism and the presence of American troops on Trinidad affected the political nature of this music in the mid twentieth century. Artists such as the Mighty Sparrow and Lord Kitchener (Aldwyn Roberts) used calypso as the voice of political change and social upheaval in the 1950s and early 1960s. Many calypso artists allied themselves with the Peoples National Movement Party, which demanded self-determination. They got their way in 1962.

The calypso is a funky style of music, though its funkiness has nothing to do with black America's funk movement in the '70s. Its funkiness is purely unique and gentler than the common American concept of funk. Make sure you bring out the accents in the hi-hat when playing the beat in **FIGURE 13-20**. Also, make sure the natural syncopation in the bass drum feels relaxed and nonmechanical. Finally, as you can see, this beat is written in 2/2 time. For more information on this time signature see Chapter 16.

Soca

While calypso may have been an instrument of political flux, soca is pure party music. Soca is largely credited to the singer Arrow (Alphonse Cassell), who was born on the nearby island of Montserrat. Arrow popularized the soca with his 1983 number one hit "Hot, Hot, Hot."

Soca is more upbeat and modern in its musical approach, and like the merengue, soca regularly uses a throbbing half note in the bass drum, giving this music its dance appeal. (See **FIGURE 13-21**.)

 FIGURE 13-20 Calypso

 FIGURE 13-21 Soca

TRACK 64

TRACK 65

FIGURE 13-22 Reggae

TRACK 66

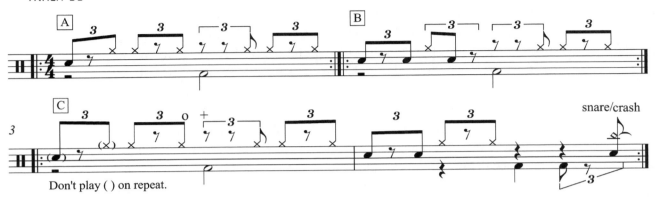

Don't play ( ) on repeat.

Today, the soca may be the defining dance music of the Eastern Caribbean, as it has given rise to a still newer offshoot called rapso, which is currently very popular. This subgenre combines the spirited nature of soca with the grittiness of American rap music.

Reggae

Like the music of Trinidad, reggae has also been the voice of social and political unrest. The late Bob Marley is probably the most famous Jamaican singer who wrote about racism and political injustice in his music.

The beats in **FIGURE 13-22** are basic reggae patterns that have a wide application. Notice how the bass drum and the snare—in this case the side stick—is the reverse of what we find in rock music. In rock, we typically hear the kick on the downbeats of one and three and the snare drum on the downbeats of two and four. Reggae, generally, works the opposite.

You'll notice that in groove B, a side stick triplet pattern has been written. Play this so that each triplet is progressively softer; this creates a nice echo effect. Also observe that with groove C, a small fill has been included at the end of measure two.

You can see that Latin music has many categories and is quite expansive. Use the appendices in the back of the book to learn more about this vibrant musical style.

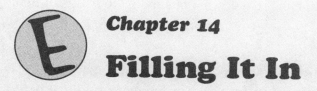

Chapter 14
Filling It In

Drumming revolves around beats, fills, and beat/fill combinations. Sometimes fills are deliberate breaks from a groove. In this case, the fill acts as segue between phrases or sections in a tune. Other times, fills are built into the groove itself and represent subtle shifts in the music. In this chapter, we will discuss both kinds of fills as they relate to rock drumming and its derivative styles.

When and Where Do I Fill?

Without belittling rock music, it's safe to say that it is the easiest style for beginners to get their hands around. Rock can be quite complex, but for our purposes, we'll keep it simple and use it as a template to learn how to play fills. Since there are many branches on the rock-drumming family tree, we will try to make the following fills meet the needs of many styles.

Deciding on a Fill

It will be up to you to decide what fill works best in a given situation. You will need to develop an ear for appropriateness and an ear for idiomatic playing. This is something a book cannot do for you. The only way to do this is to listen to as many recordings as possible and to interact with musicians.

Always seek to serve the song. Never play a fill, or a beat for that matter, just to play it. Random fills will actually interrupt a song's groove and interfere with what the other musicians are playing. No one likes being "stepped all over," as is commonly alleged by musicians who feel that somebody in the band is being musically insensitive.

When confronted with a new song, think about the tune's structure and observe the way the song builds. Choose beats and fills that you think best elevate the tune and make it a one of a kind. If it's a song that's already been recorded, listen to the CD and internalize what the previous drummer did.

In the case of previously recorded material, this does not mean that you will necessarily play the same drum part note for note. Different interpretations can be valid as long as your changes are well thought-out. The important thing is to *always* serve the song.

If you're in a working situation, assess the type of gig you're playing. If the song in question is the first dance at a wedding, recreate what you hear on the CD. If you're playing with an art rock band, then by all means, think about how you can put your stamp on the music.

Playing Idiomatic Fills

With fills, it all comes down to the type of music you're playing. If you're jamming on Jimi Hendrix tunes, you will have a great deal of freedom to fill all over the place. If you're playing in a studio session, backing up a pop singer, you'll want to play only those fills that add to the song's forward momentum. In general, studio gigs require drummers to play more conservatively. In this setting, the fills you use should be rock-solid and easy to follow.

The most common type of fill is one used in between musical phrases. Sometimes all that is needed is a cymbal crash on the downbeat of the new section. Other times, you may want to play a fill for a whole measure or longer. This type of fill seals holes in music, helping a song to flow smoothly from one section to another or one phrase to another. The name of the game here is to listen for these holes and to fill them up as you see fit. Keep in mind that you don't have to fill *every* hole. Often, it's nice to leave some open space.

Sometimes you will want to play what is called "a kick." Kicks are used to set up key rhythmical figures played by the band. When a drummer plays a kick, he or she is really prepping the band members and the listeners alike for an important rhythmic pattern. A kick is strategic, and is usually played a beat or two before the said rhythmical figure.

Kicks prep only standout or prominent rhythmical figures. Do not kick subtle rhythmic variances or you will only destroy the flow of the music. Kicks are used primarily in big band and Latin jazz, but you will find them in rock and other styles, too. For more information on this type of fill, see Appendix B.

Basic Fills on the Snare Drum

The following fills are one measure in length and can be used in almost any style of rock. In order to get the most out of these fills, first learn the pattern, and then apply it to a beat. One way to do this is to play three measures of the basic rock groove, then one measure of a fill.

When playing the basic rock beat, ride on a closed hi-hat for now. You can spice it up later.

As you come out of the fill, strike your crash cymbal on the downbeat of the next measure; this will signify the beginning of a new phrase and a return to the beat. After you strike the cymbal, make sure your ride hand returns to the hi-hat either on the *and* of one or on the downbeat of two. Always include a note in the bass drum when crashing on the cymbal.

When you play the fill itself, it's a good idea to feather the bass drum on all four downbeats and *chick* the hi-hat foot on the downbeats of two and four. This will help to stabilize the time. It also promotes four-way coordination.

Basic Eighth Note Snare Drum Fills

To start off, let's try simple eighth notes on the snare drum. (See **FIGURE 14-1**.) You should start with the right hand and alternate. When playing this kind of fill, you may want to include a crescendo. By doing this, you add expression to the music, making it sound more organic.

Sixteenth Note Snare Drum Fills

For the next fill (**FIGURE 14-2**), let's play straight sixteenth notes on the snare drum. Again, alternate and begin with the right hand. If you're feeling adventurous, try adding accents or even ghost notes.

The fills in **FIGURE 14-3** are a group taken directly from the snare drum etudes you learned in Chapters 5 and 8. This has been done to

FIGURE 14-1 Basic snare drum fill

FIGURE 14-2 Sixteenth note fill

show you the relationship between snare drumming and drum set playing. Be sure to follow any sticking indications.

Half Measure Fills

Now let's try using half measure fills since this is also quite common. The fills in **FIGURE 14-4** can be placed on any two beats within a measure. However, you will find that in a real musical situation they are best used on beats three and four. When practicing these fills, make sure you punctuate them with a crash cymbal, as you did in the previous figures. Also, make sure that you do not lose track of where you are in the four-measure phrase or in the fourth measure itself. Using a metronome will help to keep you on track.

FIGURE 14-3 Snare drum fills

TRACK 67

FIGURE 14-4   Half measure fills on the snare

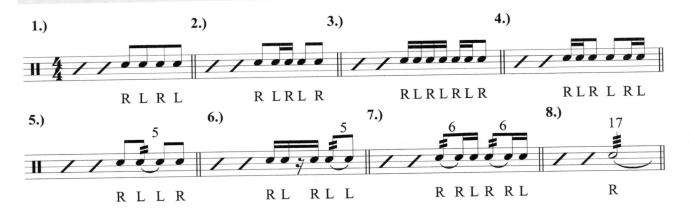

You will notice that the first two beats of each fill contain hash marks. This means to keep playing the basic rock beat until you get to beat three where the fill begins. These fills are also taken directly from the etudes in Chapters 5 and 8.

Moving Around the Set

The next batch of fills incorporates your tom-toms. These fills have been written for a five-piece kit (two rack toms and a floor tom). If you have a smaller drum set, make adjustments as necessary. For example, if you have only a 12" rack tom, take the notes written for the 13" rack tom and move them to the floor tom or the snare drum. Be creative!

Like the fills in **FIGURES 14-1** through **14-4**, the fills in **FIGURE 14-5** use basic duple subdivisions, namely, quarter notes, eighth notes, and sixteenth notes. Some of these fills also include rolls. Again, make sure you crash on the downbeat of one as you come off of the fill. Also, be sure to follow the sticking indications.

Now let's use half measure fills on beats three and four of bar four. (See **FIGURE 14-6**.) Don't forget to punctuate these fills with a crash cymbal, as you did in the previous figures. Again, make sure not to lose track of the four-bar phrasing.

FIGURE 14-5 Fills around the kit

TRACK 68

FIGURE 14-6 Half measure fills around the kit

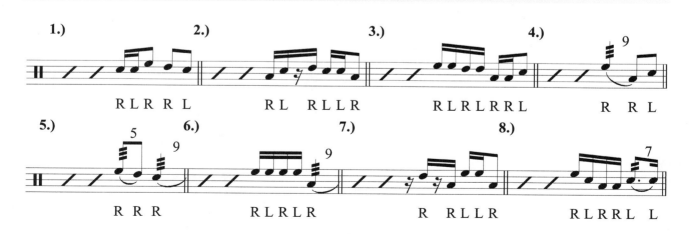

Triplet Fills Around the Set

The fills in **FIGURE 14-7** are designed to move eighth note triplets around the kit. They contain combinations of triplets, quarter notes, and eighth notes. You should practice these fills on the snare drum as preparation for playing the exercises as written.

You should also practice these fills in exactly the same manner as you practiced the other figures in this chapter.

Now try playing half measure triplet fills. (See **FIGURE 14-8**.)

FIGURE 14-7 Triplet fills around the kit

TRACK 69

FIGURE 14-8 Half measure triplet fills

Advanced Fills

The following fills are a potpourri of everything you have learned thus far plus some new twists. These fills incorporate both duple and triple rhythmic patterns and you will also see flams and ruffs in some of them. In addition, they use sixteenth note triplets, or sextuplets. Remember, six sextuplets equal one beat. Logically, then, three sextuplets equal a half a beat. Sextuplets are exactly twice the speed of eighth note triplets. You will also find trickier sticking patterns indicated here, and newest of all, you will now use the bass drum in the fill itself; the bass drum will act as another tom-tom. (See **FIGURE 14-9**.)

All of these fills are commonplace among drummers. Refer back to Chapter 9 if you are having trouble developing the technique to play these bass drum figures or if you're confused as to what foot techniques to even use. To promote four-way coordination, *chick* the hi-hat on the downbeats of two and four as you play each fill. Each fill is one measure in length.

The next group of fills (**FIGURE 14-10**) is similar to **FIGURE 14-7** except that these fills are half a measure in length and occur only on beats three and four.

On any of the preceding figures, you can substitute other, more complicated, rock beats for the basic groove you've been using. As you become comfortable with these fills, use more and more complex beats in conjunction with each figure.

FIGURE 14-9 Advanced fills

TRACK 70

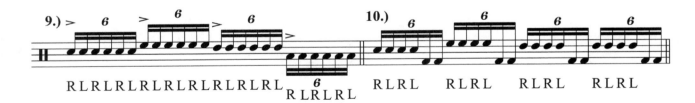

FIGURE 14-10   Advanced half measure fills

TRACK 11

1.)   2.)   3.)   4.)

R L R L   R R L L   R   R R L   R R   R R

5.)   6.)   7.)   8.)

R L L R L L   R L R L   R L R L

Beat/Fill Combinations

Beat/fill combinations occur when a drummer does not cease playing a groove in order to play a fill. Instead, the beat and fill are intertwined and there is no real separation between them. Sometimes, beat/fill combinations are difficult to detect, because they can be quite understated. There may only be a subtle shift in the groove pattern or an unexpected series of accentuations, rhythmic anticipations, or rhythmic suspensions. **FIGURE 14-11** shows a few examples of these types of beat/fill combinations.

FIGURE 14-11   Beat/fill combination

Play crash only on repeat.   beat/fill combination

FIGURE 14-12 Beat/fill combination

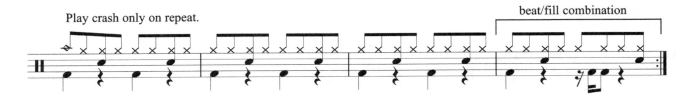

FIGURE 14-13 Beat/fill combinations using tom-toms

TRACK 72

FIGURE 14-14 Beat/fill combinations using tom-toms

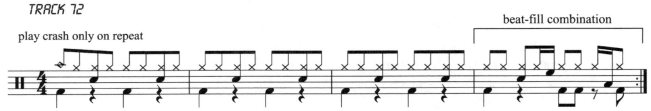

TRACK 73

FIGURE 14-15 Subtle beat/fill combination

FIGURE 14-12 is another similar type of beat/fill combination.

Beat/fill combinations can also use tom-toms, as shown in **FIGURES 14-13** and **14-14**.

Finally, beat/fill combinations can be highly syncopated but still spacious. The beat/fill combination in **FIGURE 14-15** uses one note to alter the groove. You will find a splash cymbal notated on the *e* of beat four. If you don't have a splash cymbal, strike the bell of your ride or crash.

There are many types of fills available to you. To get a glimpse of this, try figuring out all the permutations of just eighth notes on four surfaces (a snare and three toms). The possibilities are seemingly endless when it comes to playing both straight up fills and beat/fill combinations. Spend some time experimenting with your own fills.

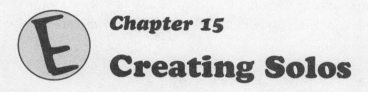

Chapter 15

Creating Solos

Soloing is one of the toughest aspects of drumming, because you have no one else to lean on. To solo well, you must have a good sense of time, structure, and, most of all, confidence. You must also be able to take one idea or a series of related ideas and develop them logically.

Telling a Story

Soloing requires a great deal of poise, and in many ways, it is the ultimate test of your technical skill and creative talents. Some drummers love to solo, while others detest it. Buddy Rich, for example, felt very comfortable soloing and was great at it. On the other hand, one of Rich's contemporaries, Dave Tough, avoided soloing, feeling that he was lousy at it. However, recordings with Woody Herman and others prove Tough's greatness, whether he recognized it or not.

On Your Own

When you solo, you are all by yourself. The entire musical load is placed on your shoulders and there is nothing or no one to hide behind. For some, this is thrilling; for others, this causes panic. If you're well prepared, though, soloing should be fun and invigorating.

Soloing is akin to storytelling. In order to tell a story, you must be an articulate speaker. This means having a good vocabulary and knowing how to apply it. All this relates to drumming. To be an articulate drummer, you need to have great stick control and four-way coordination. Once you develop a strong musical vocabulary, you will be ready to create an artistic statement.

There's just one more element to soloing: creative energy. Creative energy is difficult to define because it is highly personalized. We can say this much: It is bound by your conception of music and your conception of the instrument you play.

Developing Solos

Have you ever been to the theater? If you have, you watched characters on the stage interact in some fashion. Without a script, these characters are nameless faces; they are mute and devoid of emotion. The author's job is to infuse them with opinions, habits, susceptibilities, goals, dreams, and other personality traits. If the playwright does a good job, each character fits neatly into the storyline and each contributes to the propulsion of the plot. If the author is first-rate, you will empathize with each character's unique struggle.

It may sound silly, but think of your drums and cymbals as characters in a play. Try to bring out each drum and cymbal's individual voice and character traits. Do this through musical dialogue.

Solos can be developed in many ways. You can use theme and variation, call and response, tension and release, and so on, but no matter what structure you employ, you will need a subject or a motif to stimulate coherent dialogue. In a theatrical production, the characters must have a shared concern, otherwise they will chatter aimlessly. This shared concern is the playwright's premise, or motif. Use of a motif avoids directionless dialogue. The same is true of drumming. By using a motif, your musical dialogue will resonate deeper.

A motif is a particularly memorable riff that is used as a springboard for improvisation. You could call a motif the essence, core, or heart of a solo. You'll want to make sure that everything you play derives from a motif. As you become more advanced in your soloing, you may use a series of motifs to create a theme. For now, concentrate on only one motif and keep it simple.

How to Choose

When playing any solo, you must be able to choose motifs that best fit the music. You can easily tell the difference between a young player and a mature player by the types of motifs used and by the quantity of motifs used. Novices tend to use way too many ideas in a solo. They string together several musical non sequiturs, rather than state a premise, develop it, and move to a conclusion.

Shorter solos, such as four- and eight-bar breaks, commonly found in jazz, do not require as much formal structuring as do extended solos, as they are the result of interplay between the drummer and other soloists. But in either type of solo, motifs should be used to keep you on track and to spur you on toward meaningful improvisation.

As previously stated, musical dialogues must be logical and well organized. Let's pretend you are having a conversation with somebody named Joe. If you say, "Hey Joe, how are you doing?" And Joe responds with, "There are 2 million tribally enrolled Native Americans in the United States today," you will think poor Joe's lost his mind. This is because

Joe's response had no connection to your question. This can happen in a musical conversation, too, so you must be attentive when you solo. Listen to yourself, to the other musicians around you, and to the melody of the tune you're playing. By doing this, you will be able to contribute better to the music being rendered.

Ending Your Solo

Finally, you need to know when you've played enough—when you've told your story and you have nothing more to add. Don't reiterate solo ideas just because you feel like jibber-jabbering on the bandstand. State an idea, develop it, end it logically and climactically, then let someone else speak. Often, inexperienced soloists think that they can keep building and building their solo. Before you know it, the solo has passed its peak and the audience loses interest.

Any playwright can write Act 1, but only great writers can finish Act 2. This applies to drumming as well. Unfortunately, the answer is not simple. Knowing how and when to end a solo is something you will learn *only* through experience and by listening to other drummers. In time, you will develop an intuitive sense for this, and your solos will be a hit.

Creating Solo Motifs

Let's talk about beginning a solo. Where do motifs come from? They come from the tune you're playing. They should be rhythmic patterns that you feel comfortable with, but, most of all, they must have some relationship to the song you plan to solo over. The exercises here have been designed to help you organize and streamline your musical ideas. With this in mind, we will start with this one measure of music. (See **FIGURE 15-1**.)

FIGURE 15-1 Solo motif

Now let's orchestrate this motif around the drum set. We'll try four variations; all this will add up to one four-bar phrase. When you practice **FIGURE 15-2**—indeed all of the figures in this chapter—play your hi-hat on the downbeats of two and four with your foot.

In the **FIGURE 15-3**, we've altered, or spiced up, the motif.

Now let's try using the motif in a call-and-response discussion. Call and response is a vital part of soloing. This applies both to the extended solo format and especially to the interband-trading format. During an extended solo, you should play the role of questioner and answerer. When trading fours or eights, you should bounce ideas off of other musicians in a conversational manner.

In the **FIGURE 15-4**, you will see an eight-bar phrase. The first, third, fifth, and seventh bars contain fancy versions of the motif.

Finally, let's use our basic motif in a more advanced call-and-response setting. (See **FIGURE 15-5**.) This will be twelve bars long, which is the same length as the common blues form. Anytime you see a crash cymbal marked, you may strike either the edge of the ride or the crash. Most importantly, observe how the solo never strays too far from the main motif.

FIGURE 15-2 Motif variations

FIGURE 15-3 More motivic variations

FIGURE 15-4 More motivic variations

R L R L L R   R L R L R L R L   R L R L L R R R L

R R L   R L R L

FIGURE 15-5 Twelve-bar solo

TRACK 74

R L R L R L R   L R L R L L L R R L L L R L R

R L L R R L R   L R L R L R R L R L R L

R L R L R   L   L R L R L R R L L L L

R L R L L L R   R R L R L R R L R L R R L R

Soloing on Longer Song Forms

There are two types of extended solos: song form solos and cadenza solos. When playing either kind, you will need to use a series of motivic ideas and you will need to develop them gradually. Wide-open cadenza solos are really fun to play, because you do not have to follow a strict song structure.

When following a song structure, you must, first and foremost, not get lost. You must also cue in the listener to the tune while simultaneously disguising it. It's a bit of a contradiction. You do not want to simulate the song's melody literally, yet you will need to hint at the melody and the song structure so that your solo doesn't metamorphose into pure weirdness.

In **FIGURE 15-6**, you will see a thirty-two-bar advanced bebop solo, written in AABA form. Each section is eight measures long. The B section is commonly referred to as the bridge. Together AABA makes up one full chorus. When playing a solo in jazz, you may play as many as four or five choruses before the band resumes. Since we do not have a song to use, we will build our solo around two motifs. The first motif will represent section A. It is two measures long.

The next motif (**FIGURE 15-7**) will represent section B. It is only one bar long.

Study how the motifs have been varied in **FIGURE 15-8**. Sometimes rests have been used to elongate the motif. Other times, the motif appears shortened or sped up. Observe the phrasing, too. You will see that

FIGURE 15-6 Solo motif A

FIGURE 15-7 Solo motif B

FIGURE 15-8 Thirty-two bar bebop solo

32 Bar Bebop Solo

By Eric Starr

FIGURE 15-8 Thirty-two bar bebop solo—*continued*

three-beat phrasing has been used in both the second A section and in the last A section; this is done by shaving off a beat at the beginning or end of the motif. Three-beat phrasing creates an "over the bar line" feel; it helps to infuse the solo with tension and release, which creates suspense and momentum.

Also, observe how the final A section climaxes. The easiest way to make a solo climax is to increase the volume and to use a lot of cymbal crashes.

A cross-stick (c.s.) has been used in some of the measures and is indicated by an *x* note head. To play a cross-stick, press the tip of your left stick into the drumhead, then hit that stick with the opposite or right hand. When striking the shaft of the left stick, don't let the tip buzz on the head. In measure seven, you will notice a left-handed snare note followed by a cross stick. In order to play the cross stick in time, you will need to play the preceding snare hit using a dead stroke (see Chapter 3, Control Strokes). Also, in measure sixteen, you will see a cross-stick accompanied by a ruff. In this case, you will need to buzz the ruff in order to play the cross-stick. Do not let the left stick buzz, however, as you strike it with the right hand.

As stated for **FIGURE 15-5**, when you see a crash cymbal marking, feel free to use either the ride or the crash. Lastly, don't forget to *chick* the hi-hat on the downbeats of two and four. Ⓔ

Chapter 16

Exploring Time Signatures

So far you have played almost exclusively in 4/4. You were introduced to 3/4 in Chapter 12, but you have yet to play any odd time signatures. In this chapter, we will take a look at some common meters then dive headfirst into odd time.

Conceiving of Time Signatures

The most widely used time signatures in Western music are 4/4, 3/4, 6/8, 2/4, and 2/2; 4/4 is clearly the most universal, hence its nickname "common time." For now, though, let's leave 4/4 behind and explore some other common meters.

6/8 is employed quite often in marching band, concert band, and orchestral music. It also turns up in less formal styles of music such as the three genres we already discussed, namely, rock, jazz, and Latin.

Time signatures can be confusing to the ear. For instance, a six-beat feel can be written and conceived of in 6/8 or 6/4. It all depends on the tune being played. Usually, the difference lies in the tempo and in the phrasing. Meters also tend to give themselves away by the way the measure itself is divided. We will get to this in a moment.

The 6/8 Measure

6/8 means that there are six beats in a measure; the eighth note gets, or receives, one beat. (See **FIGURE 16-1**.)

A triple meter, as opposed to a duple meter, 6/8 is almost always divided into two equal parts. Instead of counting "one-two-three-four-five-six," which becomes quite a tongue twister at faster tempos, 6/8 is usually counted "one-two, one-two, etc." (See **FIGURE 16-2**.) Since it is a triple meter, the eighth notes feel like eighth note triplets in 4/4.

It's important to understand that, theoretically, just about any rhythm can be written in just about any way. This includes variances in both notation and time signature. For example, the two examples in **FIGURES 16-3** and **16-4** sound identical.

When played at the indicated speeds, you will not hear a difference between **FIGURES 16-3** and **16-4**. Yet, they look very different: One is written

FIGURE 16-1 6/8 measure counted in six

FIGURE 16-2 6/8 measure counted in two

using quarter notes; the other is written using eighth notes. One is written in 3/4; the other is written using a 4/4-2/4 combination. 2/4, by the way, is merely one bar of 4/4 cut in half.

As you can see, notation and time signatures can be twisted to represent just about any rhythmical idea. **FIGURES 16-3** and **16-4** teach us that notation and meter are relative and subjective. There are no ironclad rules about how to present music on paper, just as there are no "set in stone" rules about how to conceive of or feel music.

Most of the time, however, there is a preferred way to write a rhythmic pattern and the more you read music, the more you will understand the unique characteristics and demands of each time signature. You will also gradually develop an intuition for what rhythmic patterns and time signatures go best together.

Needless to say, if somebody says "play in six," you may visualize it in two different ways. You could imagine that the eighth note equals the beat, as in 6/8, or you could imagine that the quarter note equals the beat, as in 6/4. Either way, no one could categorically call you wrong since both are legitimate time signatures.

FIGURE 16-3   Quarter notes in 3/4

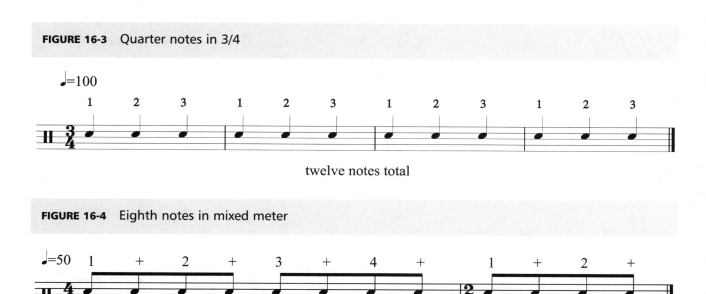

twelve notes total

FIGURE 16-4   Eighth notes in mixed meter

twelve notes total

There are some general notions about music and meter that you should follow, though. If the music you're playing is not written down, use your ears to decide what meter fits best. An easy way to discern between 6/4 and 6/8, for example, is to find the pulse of the music and gauge its speed. If you're traveling at a fast clip, you should conceive of the music in 6/8. If the six beats move slowly, it's probably best to think of it in 6/4. In the case of the latter, you could even think of it in 3/4.

Unlike 6/8, 6/4 is not very common. However, sometimes a waltz contains so many six-beat phrasings that it warrants counting it in six. Also, songwriters sometimes tag an extra two beats onto the end of a phrase of 4/4. This is usually done for harmonic reasons or to support a melodic hook. When this occurs, you have a typical 6/4 measure.

2/2 Measure

Let's move on to other meters. Common time, or 4/4, has a close relative called 2/2. 2/2 means that there are two beats in a measure; the half note equals one beat. 2/2 is called "cut time" or "fast 4," and it appears on paper to look just like 4/4.

2/2 is different from 4/4, though. It is used only for fast tempos. In 2/2, half notes are counted and played like quarter notes in 4/4; quarter notes are counted and played like eighth notes in 4/4; eighth notes are

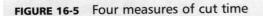

FIGURE 16-5 Four measures of cut time

FIGURE 16-6 Two measures of 4/4

counted and played like sixteenth notes in 4/4, and so on. It's helpful to see it notated (see **FIGURES 16-5** and **16-6**).

12/8 Ballad

The preceding figures illustrate the tricky nature of notation as it relates to time signatures. It's helpful to know, however, that there are some common beats associated with each time signature. In rock 'n' roll, blues, gospel, and jazz, you might hear the beat shown in **FIGURE 16-7** being played by drummers.

12/8 means that you have twelve beats in a measure; the eighth note gets, or receives, one beat. Most of the time, 12/8 is thought of as 4/4 with a triplet feel. Theoretically, it can be counted in twelve, but this is never done. It's much easier to count 12/8 in terms of 4/4.

The 12/8 ballad fits very nicely on tunes such as "Blue Moon," "Willow Weep for Me," "At Last," and others; these are all popular American standards. When playing this beat, you may ride on either the hi-hat or the cymbal. You may also use a side stick in place of a regular snare drum stroke. When riding on the cymbal, always remember to play your hi-hat foot on two and four.

FIGURE 16-7 12/8 ballad

TRACK 76

Cut Time

In cut time, or 2/2, we often find the beat in **FIGURE 16-8** being used.

This beat is used primarily in country and western, rock, and gospel music.

FIGURE 16-8 Cut time groove

TRACK 77

Sometimes this beat comes toward the end of a song, when the musicians or singers decide that they want to raise the level of excitement. To do this, the band will jump from 4/4 into double time. Double time, in this case, means 2/2. In this context, drummers will often ride on a partially opened hi-hat or even the edge of a crash cymbal. By doing this, you will get a thick wash of sound.

Odd Time Signatures

The use of odd time signatures in drum set music stems from twentieth-century so-called classical music, and from ethnic music with origins in Africa, the Middle East, and the Far East. Composers such as Alban Berg, Igor Stravinsky, Maurice Ravel, and others experimented with odd meters quite frequently. As well, traditional musicians from India, Iran, Egypt, Bali, and many other countries use variances in meter in their music.

Jazz, rock, and Latin have all given birth to subgenres of music. Many of these offshoots have divorced themselves from dance in an effort to expand the realm of musical possibilities. Typically, dance music uses only common meters such as 4/4 and 3/4, but not all musicians are content to play in these time signatures. Because of this, distinct styles of music have emerged that are strictly listener based.

FACT

The progressive rock movement was also extremely popular in the 1970s. Megastars Genesis, Yes, (Emerson, Lake, and Palmer), Rush, and others, spearheaded the movement, and all of these groups used odd time signatures extensively. Audiences flocked to see these bands play in arenas across the globe.

In jazz, pianist Dave Brubeck and others experimented with odd time signatures in the '50s and '60s. In 1959, Brubeck struck gold with the very popular "Take Five," a cool-style jazz tune by alto saxophonist Paul Desmond. On this piece, drummer Joe Morello takes a solo in 5/4 that is now considered quite legendary. On the same album, entitled *Time Out*, the Brubeck masterpiece "Blue Rondo à la Turk" appears. This song remains one of only a handful of jazz compositions written in 9/8.

The 1960s also saw the rise of avant-garde jazz being recorded on major record labels. This movement sandblasted the idea of using a time signature altogether. Later in the decade, and well into the 1970s, fusion, a combination of jazz and rock, became popular with musicians. Groups such as John McLaughlin's Mahavishnu Orchestra and Chick Corea's Return to Forever cranked up the volume, but used extremely complex musical structures; this included the use of odd time signatures.

Experiments in odd time continue to this day but on a smaller level. In general, dance and groove music still reigns, which is fine by many musicians. The main problem is that the type of music that tops the charts excludes a lot of players. Musicians find it harder to make a living as technology makes it easier for singers to work without a band or with a scaled-down group. This affects drummers, too.

The billion-dollar record industry is in a period of crisis, due in large part to the popularity of Internet bootlegging and CD Recordables. Today's focus is on expendable artists who can make a quick fiscal return. The result is corporate-driven pop, R & B, and dance music. Needless to say, odd-metered "art" rock and experimental jazz live within a much smaller market today.

However, if you're interested in creative, odd-metered music, don't despair. The history of music shows that what goes around usually comes around, so odd-metered music is likely to gain in popularity at some point.

The following pages contain exercises that have crossover value in rock and jazz. In order to best understand their applications, you will need to refer to Appendix A for listening examples. As your own playing matures, you should experiment with odd time beats and fills. Come up with your own rhythmic patterns and find other like-minded musicians who will help structure these ideas into songs. Explore, be creative, and most of all, have fun doing it.

FIGURE 16-9 2+3 rock in five

ride on hi-hat

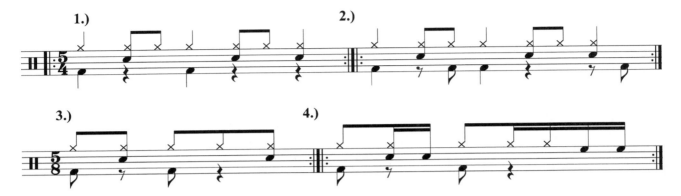

FIGURE 16-10 2+3 swing in 5/4

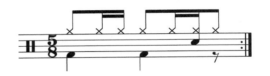

FIGURE 16-11 2+3 swing in 5/8

FIGURE 16-12 3+2 rock in five

TRACK 78

ride on hi-hat

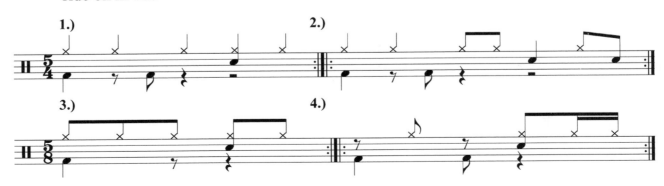

Playing in Five

Playing in "five" means playing in either 5/4 or 5/8. As previously stated, faster beat pulsations should be visualized and notated in 5/8, while slower ones are best conceived of in 5/4. When in five, you should divide the measure into two unequal parts. Use 2+3 or 3+2 measure divisions. In **FIGURES 16-9** and **16-10** you will find some examples of 5/4 and 5/8 divided using 2+3.

If a composer chooses to write a swing feel in 5/8, he or she will not want to use triplets or "swing eighth notes." 5/8 implies a swift tempo. (See **FIGURE 16-11**.) As stated in Chapter 12, at fast speeds the triplet ride pattern morphs into straight-up eighth notes.

Let's change the bar division from **FIGURE 16-11** so that we feel it 3+2. This type of bar division is more common. (See **FIGURE 16-12**.)

Now let's use a triplet, or swing, feel. See **FIGURE 16-13**.

FIGURE 16-13   3+2 swing in five

TRACK 79

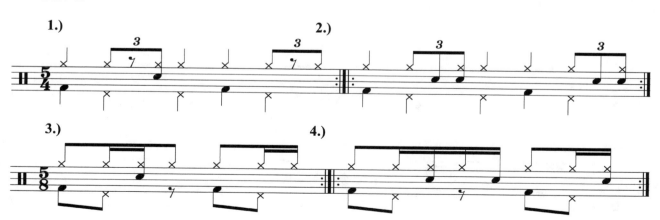

Playing in Seven

Playing in seven means that you will play either in 7/4 or 7/8. The bar will either be divided 3+4 or 4+3. **FIGURES 16-14, 16-15, 16-16,** and **16-17** will introduce you to both 7/4 and 7/8 and to both types of bar divisions. Some open hi-hat notes have also been included here.

FIGURE 16-14   3+4 rock in seven

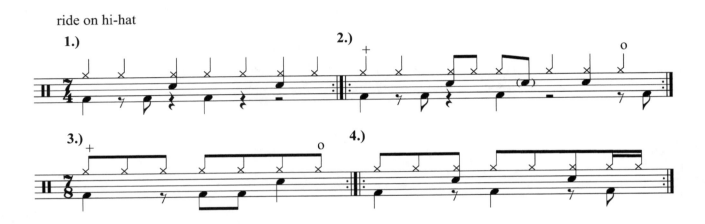

FIGURE 16-15   3+4 swing in seven

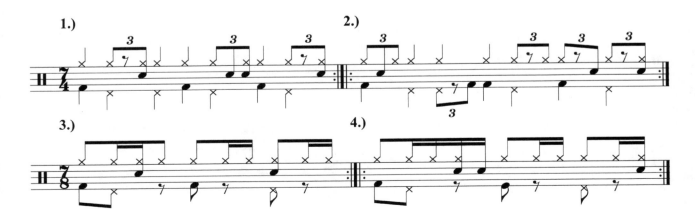

Playing in Nine

Nine is not used a lot. When it is, it is felt and notated almost always in 9/8. 9/4 is really best written in 3/4 (waltz time) or in the bimeters 4/4-5/4 or 5/4-4/4. Bimeters such as these are quite rare.

Playing in nine can be quite complicated since you now have more

 FIGURE 16-16   4+3 rock in seven

TRACK 80

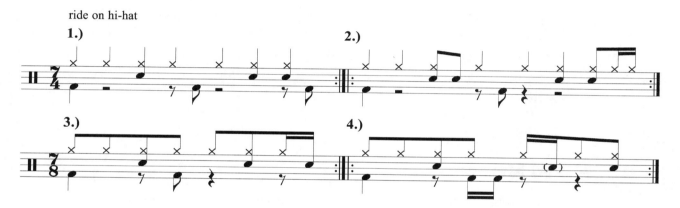

FIGURE 16-17   4+3 swing in seven

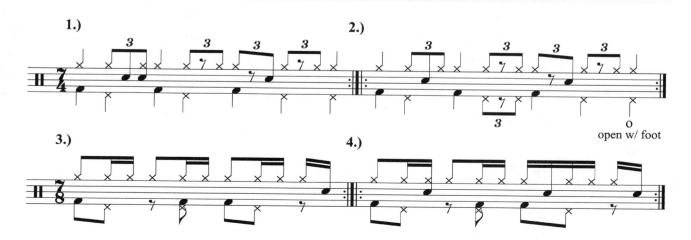

FIGURE 16-18 9/8 patterns

TRACK 81

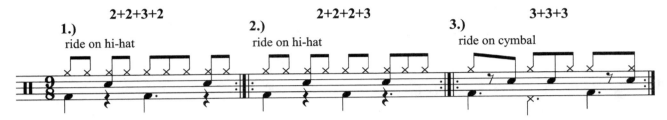

choices with regard to bar divisions. Often it is divided into small sections such as 3+2+2+2, 2+3+2+2, 2+2+3+2, 2+2+2+3, or, on occasion, 3+3+3. Let's try a few examples of 9/8. (See **FIGURE 16-18**.) The first example uses a 2+2+3+2 feel. The second example uses a 2+2+2+3 feel (like "Blue Rondo") and the last example uses a swing 3+3+3 feel. The 3+3+3 pattern really sounds like a waltz with a double-time ride pattern hovering over the top.

Mixed Meters

Mixed meters are also important to know how to play. Take any of the drum set exercises in this book and combine them as you see fit. Be creative with them. Try combining 4/4 beats with 5/4 beats, 7/4 beats with 3/4 beats. Harder still, try combining 4/4 grooves with 9/8 grooves or 7/8 beats with 5/4 beats. The difference in time signature denominators will make these beats much more challenging to play.

Multiple combinations are even more complicated. Try such combinations as 3/4, 7/8, 4/4, and 9/8. By doing this, you will create some pretty knotty rhythms—beats that are both impressive to listen to and fun to play. In general, practicing odd time signatures will improve your reading, your counting, and your sense of time.

Chapter 17

Brushes and Mallets

Brushes and mallets add greatly to the textures and colors a drummer can create on a drum set. Unfortunately, many contemporary drummers ignore brushes, feeling that they cannot be heard in loud musical environments. This is not always true, as we will get to later in the chapter. Suffice to say, brushes still have a wide range of musical applications.

Brief History of Brushes

Brushes are most often associated with jazz, although country, rock, and Latin music use them as well. Oddly enough, dirty flyswatters were the forerunner to the now elegant drum brush.

The Start of Brushing

In the second and third decades of the twentieth century, jazz drummers in New Orleans began hitting their drums with flyswatters when sticks were deemed too loud. In the swing era, the drum brush was mass-produced, and it soon became very popular with drummers. By the mid 1930s, brushes became a required item in every jazz drummer's stick bag.

Players such as Chick Webb, Dave Tough, Buddy Rich, Jo Jones, and Gene Krupa all used brushes. Little-known country swing drummers also began using them in the '30s. Until 1973, drums were not allowed at the famed Grand Ole Opry in Nashville, but, on occasion, exceptions were made and drummers graced the stage with just a snare drum and, usually, a pair of wire brushes.

Bebop jazz brought further developments to the brushes. Max Roach's brushes on "Joy Spring" from the album *Clifford Brown & Max Roach*, Roy Haynes's brush work on the ballad "Solitaire" from the album *We Three*, and Mel Lewis's brush work on "Round Midnight" from the album *Art Pepper + Eleven* are but a few examples of groundbreaking brush work from the 1950s.

The popularity of the piano trio in the bebop and cool eras also kept brushes in high demand. Key innovators were Vernell Fournier with the Ahmad Jamal Trio, and Paul Motian, Shelly Manne, Philly Joe Jones, and others with the Bill Evans Trio. Joe Morello's brush work with pianist Dave Brubeck, in a quartet setting, was also quite virtuosic.

Brushing Today

In recent years, some musicians have come to regard the brushes as something of a relic. Others have even gone so far as to say that the art form is dead. This is untrue, though many young rock drummers admittedly do not know how to use them. Today Clayton Cameron, dubbed the Brush Master, is the biggest promoter of the brushes. However, his senior contemporaries Jeff Hamilton, Kenny Washington, Lewis Nash, John Riley, and many others keep the tradition very much alive. It's safe to say brushes are here to stay.

Brushes allow a drummer to "paint" on drums and cymbals. The motions used by brush players are not dissimilar to the brush strokes used in fine art. Great musical color and texture can be achieved through the use of brushes. It could even be argued that brushes are the most expressive implement a drummer can pick up.

How Brushes Are Used

Drummers use brushes in three basic ways: They make swirls or circular patterns on their drums, they sweep across the drumhead with a side-to-side motion; and they play everything you normally would with sticks. This includes any rhythmic pattern, rudiments, grooves, accents, and so on. There are a whole host of other little tricks and sound effects that drummers use brushes for, too, but you needn't worry about them now.

People who know a little bit about brushes tend to think that brushes are limited to ballads and soft, polite music. This is untrue. Buddy Rich said that he could strike his drums with brushes as loudly as he could with sticks, and he probably could. Indeed, brushes have more musical range than they are credited with. They can be, and should be, experimented with in softer rock music passages, in folk music, in Latin grooves, and in a whole assortment of musical styles. A good brush player can also keep a band, even a seventeen-piece big band, swinging hard on up-tempo tunes. In fact, seeing a drummer do this is something not to miss! So buy a pair of brushes and experiment with them. You'll find that they offer a whole new perspective on drums and drumming.

Types of Brushes

Brushes come in a variety of shapes and styles. You can buy either the traditional wire brush or the new-fangled plastic bristle brushes. Some brushes retract into the handles to keep the bristles from getting bent or tangled. Often this is referred to as a *telescoping brush*. Handles themselves vary from metal to wood to metal with a rubber casing for ease in grip. More recently, brush offshoots have hit the market, too.

The Blastick is one such model by Regal Tip. The Blastick is somewhere in between a stick and a plastic brush. It has extra-thick plastic bristles that allow drummers who play in louder settings to get some of the same effects traditional brushes do at quieter volumes. The Blastick can be very useful, particularly in rock or country music, because it can be played louder than your average brush. You cannot create lovely circular patterns or swishes on your snare drum with this type of brush mutant, though.

Simple Brush Patterns That Really Work

There are many varieties of brush patterns. There has also been a boom in educational books and videos over the last twenty years or so, making many brush techniques readily available. Prior to this, brush instruction was learned through apprenticeship, by listening to records, and by watching bands perform live.

Because of the relative paucity of written material about brush technique, there is no "carved in stone" approach to brush playing. There tend to be highly personalized techniques that players use and pass on to their pupils.

We can, however, make some general observations about ALL good brush players. All quality brush players:

1. Use a combination of side-to-side sweeps, circular patterns, and snare drum strokes.
2. Pulse each circular pattern in time with the music.
3. Use a coated (sandpapery) head on their snare drum in order to get a good tone.
4. Use various parts of the brush to create different sounds and textures. (The tips of the bristles are used for delicate, nimble playing; the full body of the bristles is used for broad sweeps and thicker colorations; the shaft is used in conjunction with the bristles to create loud accents; the butt end of the brush is used for cymbal scrapes.)

When you practice the brushes, make sure you follow these same guidelines.

Following are a few patterns designed to induct you into the beautiful world of brushes. They are all patterns to be played on the snare drum. Feather your bass drum on all four downbeats and *chick* your hi-hat foot on the downbeats of two and four when playing each of these patterns. The only exception to this is the waltz figure.

Ballad Playing

The trickiest aspect of brush work may be in learning to play ballads. Drummers typically refer to this kind of playing as "stirring soup," because the motions you make look a lot like a person mixing potage.

In the three ballad variations following (**FIGURES 17-1, 17-2,** and **17-3**), you will notice that both hands create circles and/or swirls on the drumhead's surface. Some of the circles move clockwise; others move counterclockwise. Be sure to follow the arrows indicated in the patterns carefully.

Learn each ballad pattern one hand at a time, then combine them together gradually. Your goal should be to create an even, silky tone on the snare drum. There should be no interruptions in the sound flow. If you find that your tone is coarse or

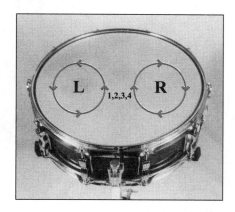

FIGURE 17-1
Brushes ballad pattern A

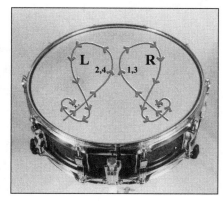

FIGURE 17-2
Brushes ballad pattern B

FIGURE 17-3
Brushes ballad pattern C

TRACK 82

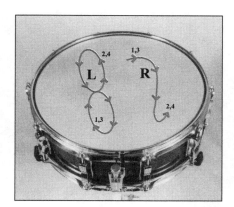

bumpy, you're probably pressing down too hard on the head. Use the tips of the bristles to get a refined sound. Finally, be certain to use large circles; make use of the full diameter of the drum.

Medium Tempo

When playing in this tempo range, you will play two different motions with your hands. Your left hand will create either a circular pattern, as in pattern A shown in **FIGURE 17-4**, or a side-to-side swish pattern, as in pattern B shown in **FIGURE 17-5**. Your right hand will strike the drum, just as you would with a stick. The rhythm played with the right hand is the basic jazz ride pattern. Make sure your hands work in harmony with each other to create a smooth, lilting swing.

FIGURE 17-4
Midtempo
brush
pattern A

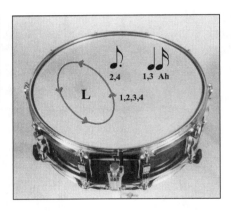

FIGURE 17-5
Midtempo
brush
pattern B

TRACK 83

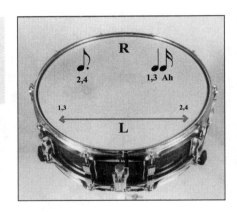

FIGURE 17-6
Up-tempo
pattern

TRACK 84

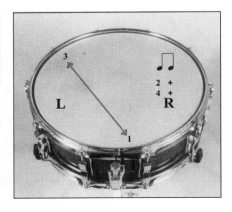

Up Tempo

You may use pattern B from **FIGURE 17-2** on up-tempo tunes. However, at blazing speeds, you probably won't be able to maintain it smoothly. The pattern in **FIGURE 17-6** can be used on even the fastest charts. It uses a back-and-forth swish movement in the left hand followed by two sixteenth notes in the right.

Waltz Time

In **FIGURE 17-7** you will see a very basic waltz pattern. This pattern is essentially the same as pattern A from **FIGURE 17-1** but with beat four missing. Feather your bass drum on beat one, and *chick* your hi-hat on beats two and three.

The "Train" Rhythm

The train rhythm is probably the easiest of the brush patterns found in this book, because you do not "stir soup" in any way. In fact, you strike the snare drum just as you would with sticks. This pattern is used mostly in country music. (See **FIGURE 17-8**.) It simulates the standup bass "slap" pattern that is commonly used in bluegrass and traditional country music.

The Rattlesnake

The Rattlesnake is a term I use to mean a trill. In this case, a trill is a fluttering sound made by playing rapid-fire sweeps with a brush; this can be done with either the right or left hand. The sound of the brush trill is similar to the sound of a prairie rattler, hence its name.

The trill can be very effective on all tempos but particularly on ballads. In **FIGURE 17-9** you will see the basic pattern, followed by a ballad pattern that uses the trill. Unlike many of the other patterns you've

FIGURE 17-7 Waltz pattern	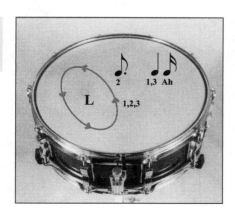

FIGURE 17-8
Train pattern

TRACK 85

FIGURE 17-9
Brush trill

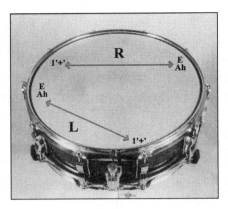

TRACK 86

learned, the trill uses only a small area of the drumhead. Using the matched grip, the only way to get this sound is to use a quick back-and-forth movement with your wrist. You'll need to turn your hand in a thumbs-up position to allow the brush to move side to side.

Use of Mallets on Drums and Cymbals

Mallets are traditionally used by percussionists who play in orchestras and/or chamber groups. However, there is no reason why you can't incorporate them into drum set music. Mallets sound beautiful on cymbals and drums alike, especially when they are used to create dynamic swells or when they are used to add sustain and coloration to the music. Mallets tend to create an eerie aura around music and, in the appropriate setting, add natural tension and release to the music.

Mallets have little use on a snare drum when the strainer is turned on. However, a snare turned in the off position makes the drum much more mallet friendly. In this case, you can use mallets to roll on your snare and tom-toms; this makes the music rumble nicely. You can even use mallets to make the music become quite thunderous!

Mallets sound particularly nice on contemporary jazz ballads, and drummers such as Elvin Jones, Art Blakey, and Tony Williams have all used them very effectively in these environs. On a ballad, mallets can be used to foreshadow and elevate dramatic endings and other climaxes.

Rolling with Mallets

When rolling on drums and cymbals, mallets also fill up space in rubato, or free music. Rubato means that the music has no set tempo or even a pulse. Lastly, mallets sound great on tunes that call for "jungle" grooves. By using the mallets as you would your sticks, you can create hypnotic rhythms on your tom-toms.

FACT

Orchestral percussionists will tell you that you should never play double stroke rolls with mallets. You needn't be this strict when playing the drum set. Clean double stroke rolls on a snare drum or high tom-tom, for example, sound great.

When you roll on cymbals or lower-pitched tom-toms, however, you should use only a single-stroke sticking. When doing this, make sure you do not roll too fast. Low tom-toms and cymbals have a lot of sustain. If you roll too fast, you're liable to choke the sound. Instead, use a medium-speed sixteenth note pattern and listen to the sound you're creating. If you hear the sixteenth notes poking through a little bit, you're probably playing at the right speed. The sixteenths will quickly lose their definition as the sound floats out toward the listener. When playing single strokes at the right speed, a listener sitting only a few feet away will hear nothing but the smooth sustain of the drum or cymbal.

Don't Be Afraid to Experiment

Pick up a pair of medium-hard tympani mallets and try them out on your kit. See what colors and textures you can come up with. Also, listen for use of mallets on recordings and watch for drummers using them in live situations. Learning to use mallets is well worth your time, because mallets will open up your ears to the rich pallet of sounds available on your drum set.

Chapter 18

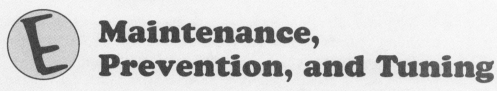

Maintenance, Prevention, and Tuning

In this chapter, you will learn some practical information about maintaining and protecting your drums. Using real-life scenarios, you will learn how to avoid having your equipment damaged, lost, or stolen. At the end of the chapter, you will also learn how best to approach tuning your drums.

Taking Care of Your Equipment

Taking care of drums, cymbals, hardware, and other drum accessories comes down to common sense. For the most part, if you treat your equipment right, it should last you a lifetime. Buying expensive new gear should only be the result of a desire to upgrade, not the result of poor instrument management.

If you're like most people, you've done something absent-minded. Maybe you lost your car keys or left your bankcard in the ATM. Who hasn't left their brown-bag lunch on the kitchen counter at home?

There is probably no working musician who hasn't had something break during a performance or left something behind after a gig. As a drummer, you are usually one of the last to leave after a show. It's not uncommon to see sheet music, a stray stand light, or some other small article left behind by the other musicians, who are in a rush to get home or to another gig. Don't let this be you.

It is ordained by life that you will make some mistakes and unwise decisions. But with regard to your drumming career, minimize distressful and forgetful moments by following some basic commonsense guidelines.

Keeping an Eye on Your Gear

First of all, if you take your equipment outside of your home, keep a close eye on it. Second, if you decide to store your drums where you're not, make sure they're in good hands.

Let's look at this common scenario: You're going over to your friend Jay's house with your drums, and you're going to jam in his basement. Perhaps you plan on leaving your gear set up at Jay's for a few days.

Think to yourself, "Is there any hazard in leaving my drums?" In any situation there is the potential for disaster. Consider all possible calamities. Ask your buddy if his basement ever floods. Ask him if he has little brothers or sisters. Young children can do a world of damage.

Are these kids going to play with your drums? Are they going to get jelly or chocolate or some other goop all over your equipment? Are they going to take markers and draw on your drumheads? Worse yet, are they going to use basement tools to bang on your drums? These are very real concerns and you will have to make a judgment call.

Also, consider the neighborhood your buddy lives in. Does he live in a seedy area of town? If so, are you confident that his house is secure? A little forethought goes a long way.

Caring For Your Drums on a Gig

Here's another scenario: Let's say you're performing at a rock club. Do you feel safe leaving equipment at the club while you go and eat dinner with the rest of the band? Is it safe to even leave your equipment in the back room while you chat with friends at the bar?

Rock clubs, indeed all clubs, are potential hazards. Most rock clubs book a lineup of bands each night and time slots are given to each group. Band X plays for forty-five minutes, the stage is quickly struck, and then the next band comes up followed by yet another band, and so on. The evening's bill may include as many as ten bands, especially if it's some sort of festival or benefit concert.

Musicians will be carting equipment in and out of the club often in assembly line fashion. Usually, the backstage area of a rock club is a whirlwind of activity. To make things more complicated, there is usually only one spot in the club where musicians pile up gear. Often, drum cases and cymbals bags are jumbled together, along with guitars, speaker cabinets, personal wardrobe, and so on.

Of course, you need to know the look of your gear from afar. Drum cases tend to make everybody's equipment look identical. It's a good idea to place brightly colored stickers on your cases so that your gear doesn't get mixed in with that loud metal drummer who played before you. Also, include a tag on all of your cases indicating your name, address, and telephone number.

You don't need to be a rocket scientist to calculate that this environment equals trouble. The good news is that rarely do musicians purposely steal equipment from other bands, but mistakes do happen.

In a situation like the one just described, watch your gear with an eagle eye. If you have other responsibilities such as greeting friends, first make sure that your equipment is safe and secure. If you absolutely must leave your drums' side, don't go too far and check back about every five minutes.

When you're at a club, survey the scene. Always ask yourself, "Are there back exits to the club?" If so, be extra-careful since, as mentioned, equipment will be going in and out. If there is no back exit, but you need to say hello to Uncle Gary, who is sitting in the corner, keep one eye on the front door to watch what comes in and what goes out. Again, this is just common sense.

Protecting Your Equipment from Others

Here's another scenario out on the street: Often, you're playing a small dinner club or restaurant that does not have a stage. In this setting, your drums may be set up very near the audience. Your average John or Jane Doe typically thinks drums are cool instruments. In fact, many of them don't hesitate to pick up a stick to whap a cymbal or tom-tom. Drunken patrons are particularly prone to this kind of behavior. Occasionally, a stranger will even sit down at your kit and begin flailing away.

Don't tolerate this behavior. Politely ask the person not to touch your drums and hold out your hand to take the sticks away from them. If they give you a hard time, contact the restaurant manager. Patrons must learn that touching any instrument, without the consent of its owner, is inappropriate. Unfortunately, it's your job to teach these curious passersby one by one.

ALERT!

If you're leaving your gear in a parked car, be very careful. It is not recommended to do this ever, but if you must, make sure not only that the car is locked, but that your gear is not visible. Always try to fit as much equipment as possible in a locked trunk. If you need to, prioritize. Make sure smaller items that can be easy to grab and run with are locked in the trunk. If you're going out to an all-night diner after a gig, request a window seat and park your car so that you can watch it from the table. Car alarms and tinted glass also reduce theft.

Drums, Cymbals, and Hardware Maintenance

The next big question is "How do I protect my drums from myself?" There are some simple rules to live by that will minimize cracks, stripping, warping, and so on. There are three situations that put your gear in danger: transporting them, setting them up, and, of course, playing them.

Percussion instruments are pretty sturdy instruments. However, they are far from invincible. Bass drums are particularly vulnerable because they are often fitted with wooden hoops and are large, heavy drums. If you are carrying your bass drum in a case over your shoulder and you drop it, chances are the hoop will crack. Considering this, a hard plastic case is best suited for your bass drum even though this will make the drum considerably more bulky.

Driving Around with Your Drums

As stated earlier, cars are problematic, too. In addition to theft concerns, you need to worry about the weather. If the weather is really hot, a parked car becomes a greenhouse. Leaving drums in an extremely hot car could cause plastic veneers on your drums to peel off and/or crack.

Packing your drums in a car or in storage without cases can also be a problem; the most obvious reason being that drum shells could get nicked up. However, carrying your drums around without cases can also be perilous for your bottom snare drumhead. This head is ultrathin and a bass drum spike or cymbal stand can easily pierce through the Mylar, rendering the drum useless until you buy another head. So if you plan on taking your drums en route, get cases.

Humes & Berg makes great bags called Tuxedo Bags. They also make lightweight vulcanized fiber cases that are more durable than a gig bag. Anvil Cases offers the most durable case of all. These are virtually indestructible and are great for drummers who need to take their gear on airplanes, and the like. The downside is that they are very heavy.

While cases are necessary for the working drummer, they can be a bit hazardous to bass drum pedals and hi-hat stands. Hardware, for one, is very heavy. As you drive, items tend to shift around. For this reason, incorrectly storing bass drum pedals and hi-hat stands in hardware bags can cause the footboard stabilizer rod on the bass drum pedal and/or the foot pedal linkage rod on the hi-hat pedal to crack if you don't unclip them before placing them in the case. The worst feeling is showing up at a gig and realizing that something is broken, so make sure you're careful. It's a good idea to put your bass drum pedal on top of all the other stands in your hardware bag or case. This will protect it from getting crushed by heavier, double-braced cymbal and snare stands, and the like.

Careful Setup

The way you set up your drums also promotes or prevents damage to your equipment. One common mistake is placing your snare drum too close to your 12" rack tom-tom. Since this tom-tom hovers over the snare drum at a slightly higher level, the rim of the snare drum, if too close, will rub up against the tom-tom as you play. Heavy playing will cause your whole drum kit to shake a little. If your snare drum is touching the 12" tom-tom, it will scrape the varnish off the drum and even cut into the wood of the drum itself. When playing, always be sure to watch for this; back up your snare drum immediately if you see this occurring.

Playing Shouldn't Be Damaging

Cymbal setup is a common problem with inexperienced players. Any drum shop owner will tell you stories of guys coming in with huge chunks taken out of the cymbals or cracks that fan out across the full diameter of the cymbal. This is usually due to an improper approach toward striking the cymbal, an inappropriate stick choice, and/or an awkward cymbal setup.

Cracking a cymbal or two is expected in the career of any drummer. However, players that complain that they have to buy new cymbals every couple of months should take a step back and read the writing on the wall. Cymbals, by and large, are tough instruments. They should provide years of use if you treat them well.

If you are playing extremely loud music, raise your cymbals high enough so that you can strike them on the edge multiple times; this means having the ability to make a nice, clean hit even as the cymbal bobs downward. Your ability to "get under" the cymbal will allow you to play loud, articulate crashes without having to clobber the cymbal with all your might.

Using an appropriate stick will affect your cymbal longevity, too. Over the last ten years or so, a number of specialty sticks have come out on the market. Some of these sticks are made of plastic and metal or a combination of the two. *Only* wooden drumsticks should be used, as they help to take the burden off of each crash. After multiple uses, wooden sticks begin to break down and chip. This is actually good! You want to use a stick that is durable but has some give.

Metal sticks are particularly murderous to cymbals. Most companies that make metal sticks claim that they're to be used only for practice pads. Unfortunately, some inexperienced players think that they can use them to play louder or to play beats that are "more phat." This is pure silliness. Metal sticks will not only prematurely destroy drumheads by putting huge dents in them; they will demolish your cymbals!

The Wing Nut

Lastly, the most notorious error is fastening the wing nut down too tightly on your cymbal tilter. If you do this, the cymbal will have limited ability to waver and dip as you strike it. Not only will this choke the sound of the cymbal, it will interfere with the cymbal's ability to endure the impact of the stick. This is the number one reason why drummers crack cymbals.

For general cymbal health, keep the wing nut loose on top of the cymbal, use a washer and felt pad under the cymbal, and make sure you place a nylon or rubber sleeve on the threaded portion of the cymbal arm; this is the very tip of the cymbal stand that touches the cymbal itself. You never want metal on metal. If you don't use a sleeve, the cymbal will not only rattle on the stand, it will become, as drummers call it, "key-holed." This means that the center hole of the cymbal will wear down and resemble an old-fashioned keyhole on a door.

Hardware health is also important. Hardware can become stripped if you're wrenching the wing nuts and other various screws too tightly. Most drummers consistently do this for fear that a cymbal or a tom-tom is going to come crashing down while they play. This is mostly paranoia.

A basic rule of thumb is that if you're having trouble loosening your wing nuts as you pack up your gear, you're probably screwing them on too tightly. Sometimes stands stick and need a little tap with a drumstick, but this should not be an everyday, every time occurrence. Also, if you start seeing dents in the stand where the screw twists into the metal tubing, or if chrome has flaked away where the screws dig into the stand, you're probably giving it too much elbow grease. In general, your stands will have a much longer lifespan if you're gentle with them.

Heads, Sticks, Brushes, and Mallet Health

Heads, sticks, brushes, and mallets are all items that you will need to replace from time to time. If you are a hard-hitting rock drummer, and you're quite active, you will go through sticks pretty fast. An active rock drummer will also go through heads relatively quickly. For this kind of player, top heads on tom-toms will probably need to be changed about every three or four months; snare drumheads may need to be changed even more frequently. Extremely active professionals, such as touring drummers, change their heads as much as two or three times a week. Of course, these are guys who have endorsements and drum techs, so it's no sweat off of their back. You do not need to change your heads this often.

Obviously, if you're playing at softer volumes or if you are not very active, your heads will last longer. Jazz drummers may even use the same tom-tom heads for years, though this may be more out of laziness. No matter what style of music you play, you shouldn't be breaking heads often. Every rock drummer has broken a few snare drumheads; some have even pounded through their bass drumhead. But just like cymbal cracks, tearing heads on a regular basis should be a sign that something in your playing and/or setup isn't right.

When to Change Heads

You will know when the snare drumhead needs changing when the white batter starts to flake off and you see a translucent spot in the middle of the drumhead. For jazz players, you will know it's time to change your snare head when it starts to blacken or when the coating loses its sandpapery feel; playing with brushes causes this to happen.

You will know when tom-tom heads need replacing by the look as well as the sound of the head. As the head deteriorates, you may start to see dents or scrapes. With double-ply heads, such as the Remo pinstripe, the tone of the drum will become noticeably affected, too. If your once-lovely sounding tom-tom becomes dead or muffled, it may be because the head has suffered one too many fills.

Replacing Drumsticks

Drumsticks usually wear in three places. If you use wooden-tipped sticks, the tip will eventually start to splinter. This happens more with jazz drummers. Rock drummers who use wooden tips don't usually have this problem because their sticks get chewed up in other areas long before the tip begins to splinter. For rock players and other hard-hitters, the shafts of their sticks begin to peel in the areas where the stick comes into contact with the edges of crash cymbals and where you play rim shot backbeats on the snare drum.

One way drummers can extend the life of their sticks is to wrap a little black electrical tape around the areas of the stick that are vulnerable; do not put tape on the tip, though. Most importantly, as you see your sticks deteriorate, throw them out and buy new ones. Splintered tips don't sound as crisp and articulate on cymbals, and sticks that are severely peeling can actually become dangerous projectiles. If a stick breaks, a sharp sliver of wood could hit you in the face. This rarely happens, but it's something to be aware of.

Brush Health

Brushes usually have a long lifespan. The best way to ensure this is to buy telescoping brushes, since this will protect them during transport. If the tips of the bristles become bent or tangled, or if some of them fall out, you need to buy a new pair. Mallets should also have a long lifespan. Replace them only when the felt beater starts to deteriorate and fall off. When this occurs, you will see the plastic or wooden core poking through.

Tuning Your Drums

Learning how to tune your drums is crucial. Drums can be stubborn instruments, but with a little know-how, you can make even a cheaply made instrument sound good. The three types of drums you need to know how to tune are the tom-toms, the snare drum, and the bass drum.

How to Tune

There are some basic rules of tuning that apply to all drums. If you're putting a new head on a drum, you first want to remove the drum from the kit so that you can work more efficiently, and so you don't get a sympathetic ring from the other drums as you tap and listen to the drum's pitch.

Using a drum key, remove the old head, then use a dry rag to wipe off any debris or dust that has accumulated around the inside of the shell and along the drum's bearing edge. Place the drumhead on the shell and spin it to make sure that the lip of the head hangs evenly over the drum. Next, place the counter-hoop or rim over the drumhead and make sure it also sits evenly on top of the drum. If you find that the hoop is warped or bent, you need to buy a new one. Bent hoops cannot fasten a head to a drum very well. The result is a terrible sound and a great deal of frustration when tuning.

After you've placed the hoop on top of the head, screw in the tension rods using your fingers. At this point, the head has been seated properly on the drum and you are ready to begin tuning. Pick any tension rod, and with a drum key, turn the rod clockwise two 360-degree rotations. Now go to the rod directly *opposite* the one you just turned, and twist it also two 360-degree rotations. Next, go to the tension rod either to the right or left of the original rod and turn it two full revolutions; then move to the rod on its opposite side and twist it two full rotations. Continue this process until each tension rod has been turned two clockwise 360-degree revolutions.

Make sure you always tune using opposites, and make certain you turn each rod equally. This is the key to your tuning success. See the diagram in **FIGURE 18-1** for reference. You'll notice that the arrows show you the correct way to move from rod to rod.

As you tune, you may hear a crackle noise. Don't worry about this. This is just the sound of the Mylar film being stretched. After you've turned each rod twice around, begin the process again. Only, now you will need to use your judgment. At this point you will start to feel head resistance, so try twisting each rod only *one* full turn, then evaluate. Strike the drum softly to see where you are in the tuning process. If the head is still quite floppy and has a warbled sound, you need to keep tightening in full rotations. If it's becoming taut, you may only want to use half or quarter rotations. Remember, though, whatever you do to one rod, you must do to all of them.

Fine Tuning and Pitch Concerns

Once the drum begins to resemble a pitch, you've entered into the subjective phase of tuning and also the stage where drums begin to differ. However, before you start thinking about how high or low you want a drum's pitch to be, you will need to check your tuning accuracy.

The only way to do this is to very softly tap around the edges of the drumhead. Tap alongside each rod and listen to the pitch. Sometimes the drum's overtones are distracting when doing this. If you're having trouble discriminating between a pitch and an overtone, press slightly in the middle of the head while tapping. By doing this, you will hear a clearer fundamental pitch.

If your taps all have the same pitch, you've done a great job. If you find that your taps produce pitch variations, you need to even them out. In order to even out a drum's pitch, decide which pitch is most prevalent, then work to make each tuning area an exact match.

It's easier to hear higher pitches on a drum, so if anything, tune the drum high at first. You can always detune later. The important thing is to get the drum in tune with itself—to compass it up properly. Once you've done this, you can worry about how high or low the overall pitch should be.

If you do have pitch variances, and you are tightening or loosening individual tension rods, make sure you tap in each affected area after each turn. You will need to keep close tabs on what you're doing. If you find that you cannot even out the pitch by tightening or loosening a certain tension rod, listen to the rod's counterpart. Often that rod may be the culprit. Remember, the head is stretched onto the drum by opposing forces.

Adjusting a Drum's Sound

Once the drumhead is in tune with itself, you can begin to think about what kind of sound you want to produce. Do you want the drum to be high and poppy or low and punchy? Maybe you want it somewhere in between the two.

This is when you need to pay attention to the bottom head and its interaction with the top head. Improper tuning of the bottom head will interfere with your ability to make your drum sound good. In general, you want to keep your bottom head tighter than the top head. The initial stick attack, or ictus, comes from the top head as it is struck, but the bottom head creates most of the drum's tone.

To find the proper spread between the top and bottom heads, some drummers think in terms of conventional pitch intervals. The most popular drum interval seems to be the perfect fourth. If you go up to a piano and play middle C then an F above it, you've just played a perfect fourth. In an attempt to take the guesswork out of tuning, a lot of drummers have experimented with exact intervals such as the perfect fourth to help them tune faster and more efficiently. For example, some players tune their snare drum to an A, then tension their 12" rack tom-tom and their floor tom-tom a perfect fourth apart.

The rest of the drums should be ordered so that the smallest drum is highest in pitch and the largest drum is lowest in pitch. Given this, the bass drum will be your lowest-pitched instrument.

However, drums don't always react well to tempered tuning. They are not specific-pitched instruments by nature. If you want, play around with exact-pitched tuning, but don't get hung up on it. It's best to let the drums dictate their pitch to you. As you get to know your kit, you should start to notice that each drum has an individual voice and a preferred pitch—a kind of comfort zone. When you find this pitch, the drum will sing quite nicely.

When thinking about the pitch ranges of your drums, think high to low between the tom-toms and the bass drum; the snare drum exists in its own world. On the snare, you may want to tune the head to be either crisp and snappy or fat and sloppy. It's all up to you. However, when you tune the snare, make sure you turn the strainer to the off position so that you can hear the fundamental pitch of the drum, not the buzz of the snare wires.

The Bass Drum

Beware of the bass drum. As you tighten the tension rods, the pitch actually gets lower. This is antithetical to everything we know about tightening a drumhead. However, when the bass drum is tensioned loosely, the head is too relaxed to create much of a tone; it sounds more like a shallow box and you hear only the ugly, high-pitched overtones resonating from the beater side of the head. As you tighten the rods, the drum begins to produce a deep humming tone as both heads interact. Like your other drums, the nonbeater head should be tuned higher than the beater side.

Dampening

A related aspect of tuning has to do with dampening, or muffling, your drums. If you know how to tune your drums well, you shouldn't have to use much dampening. In fact, you should only need to pad the bass drum. The snare drum and tom-toms shouldn't need wads of tape or dishtowels wrapped around them to take away unwanted overtones and ring.

If you do have a lot of nasty overtones, it's probably because you do not have the head in tune with itself. If you have excessive ring, the bottom head is probably too loose or both heads are too loose. Never try to get rid of ring altogether. Having some ring is good; this is the way a drum naturally sounds. If you choke off a drum's resonance completely, i t will lack tone and color.

FACT

The bass drum should have a few strips of foam or even a thin pillow inside it to control the tone and to give you punch. Again though, do not muffle the drum completely. Let it breathe; let its fundamental pitch be heard.

The most important part of tuning revolves around using your ears. You need to be able to discern between pitches and tone colors. If you have trouble doing this, familiarize yourself with the piano and practice listening to and singing various intervals. Even though drums are not pitch-specific, you need to be able to hear the difference between high and low pitches. When you tune your drums, you are looking for pitch and tonal clarity. If you have a good ear for this, you will make your drums sound wonderful, and as you gain experience, you will be able to get good sounds much more quickly.

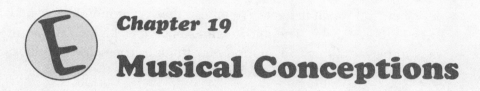

Chapter 19

Musical Conceptions

This chapter is made up of three parts. The first section gives you a conceptual framework for music making. The second part explores creativity and music from both an intellectual and a spiritual standpoint. The last section revolves around finding and maintaining joy in the music you play.

Complexity to Simplicity (Not the Other Way Around)

The great rock drummer Neil Peart once remarked that great drummers make complex music seem simple, while poor drummers make simple music seem complex. Truer words were never spoken.

When you watch first-rate drummers, there is tremendous fluidity and grace in their playing. The music seems effortless. It's very inspiring to watch a player of this caliber. You may think to yourself, "That looks simple. I can play that, too." When this happens, you've come under the spell of a gifted performer.

As you approach music and drumming, walk the road that will take you from complexity to simplicity. In order to do this, you need to understand what this really means. At first blush, such a concept may seem backward, but it's really not.

On the other hand, when you hear a beginner play, even basic beats sound awkward and forced, and nothing meaningful is communicated to you. Why does this occur? This happens because the drummer is not yet able to piece together the various complex components of music. The result is a disjointed mess.

Advancing in Skill

All drummers begin with the rudiments then advance, step-by-step, toward harder material. This is paralleled in school. For example, you learn to count before you add; you learn long division before you are taught algebraic equations, and so on. It would seem that progress itself is a gradual shift from simplicity to complexity. But, in fact, this is not entirely true—conceptually speaking, anyway.

The concept presented here is not linear. Rather, it's circular. Poet T. S. Eliot wrote, "In the end of all our exploring [we] will . . . arrive where we started . . . and know the place for the first time." This applies to music.

All musicians start out as simple listeners. However, you lose this innocence the minute you pick up an instrument and begin to explore your relationship with it. The act of learning an instrument means that you will have to tackle music's inherent complexities. If you're good, you will get your hands around these complexities, but your journey doesn't end until you land right back where you started: embracing and examining the simple splendor of a tune. In this sense, the only difference between the beginner and the pro is that experience allows the professional to see this simplicity in a whole new light.

In the context of this writing, the word *simple* has no relationship to that which is sophomoric or crude. It means that which is clearly communicated; it can still be an advanced or sophisticated idea. When you articulate music clearly, you strip it of its pretense and submit only pure ideas to an audience. There is no decoration or embellishment thrown in with the package. There is nothing superfluous or excessive in the delivery. When you present pure musical statements to a listener, you are offering musical truth. Musical truth is simple.

Grow as You Learn

As you learn new material—whether it be a snare drum etude, a drum set groove, or even a full-fledged solo—try to make that which is complicated flow from you simply. This is easier said than done, but to conceive of music this way encourages organic playing.

If you overplay, the music will be less meaningful to a listener. Overplaying does not serve the song; it only serves the ego. Remember: Less can be more!

When musical ideas are presented simply, they make more sense to a listener. This happens because the listener is not being force-fed a lot of extraneous notes. Good performers know how to take even the most sophisticated or knotty piece and make it resonate simply. This is done by stressing the music's core.

Where Does Technique Fit In?

If an average guy hears a concert violinist, he will be swayed by the passion of the music, not the complexity of the bowing or the speed of the violinist's left hand. It is doubtful that he will care one bit about the mechanics of playing the violin. He will either enjoy the performance or he won't. What is the moral of this story?

When you create music, make sure that technique is subservient to the music being produced. Make sure you keep your eye on the overall picture and put yourself in the shoes of the listener. If you're performing live, recognize that the listener doesn't care about how fast you can play a paradiddle or how accurately you can play polyrhythms. The listener only wants to be entertained and emotionally stimulated.

Music can evoke a whole litany of emotions. For example, it can sound humorous, angry, or sad. Musicians sometimes find they are bored or burned-out because they have forgotten how to listen to music like a fan of music.

Musicians examine technique, get hung up on complex details, and often forget why they began playing in the first place. That said, it is *not* recommended that you glaze over the intricacies of music making. You *do* need to examine the mechanics of music if you are to be a formidable drummer. But recognize that this is only the prep work. The test is all in how you internalize these elements, group them, and then present them to an audience.

Why You Should Disguise Complexity

For the lay public, music that sounds complex usually bores them. The actual sophistication of the music is not at issue here. Again, it comes down to the skill and maturity of the performer. If the music sounds complex, it may be because it's being played by somebody who is not good enough to make the music speak emotionally and simply. When music's complexities are exposed, a song will sound clinical and unappealing. When these complexities are disguised, the music suddenly becomes expressive and inviting.

Great musicians know this intuitively. For example, clarinetist Benny Goodman played solos that were harmonically and rhythmically complex, and the technique he employed was truly unparalleled. However, his popularity with lay audiences was not due to "chops" alone; it was the result of his ability to transform skill into energy, emotion, and excitement.

Occam's Razor

A good screenwriter knows the rule of Occam's razor (also called the principle of parsimony). This means that you state a premise and see it through logically; you don't add extraneous fluff to your work and you don't get sidetracked along the way.

Any screenwriter will tell you that dialogue must appear natural and spontaneous. Audiences will never accept dialogue that is forced and clunky. Knowing this, the writer will edit and pare down the dialogue until only its essentials remain. In other words, all unnecessary words will be "shaved off." The process the writer undergoes is extremely complex, yet the end result is often a simple conversation between two people. In order to engage an audience, the author knows that his or her delivery must be simple and coherent. The process of turning a musical idea into a usable, artistic statement is no different.

Learn to trim the fat in your playing. Make sure your concept is simple and streamlined. Don't be afraid to edit out extraneous ideas even if you love them, and, above all else, serve the needs of the music.

The Intellect versus the Spirit

How do you turn a raw musical idea into a streamlined statement? You do this by using a combination of intellect and spirit. Musical ideas stem from many sources. It's difficult to say why someone is motivated to create music. There are simply too many factors at play. Perhaps the *why* is not as central as the *how*, anyway.

There are essentially two schools of thought on how music is created.

Indeed, this applies to all art. One idea is rooted in globalism, while the other concentrates on the inner self. One idea focuses on the interconnectedness of all life, the other on personal autonomy. Both have intellectual and spiritual components.

Some musicians see creativity as a result of a collective unconsciousness, or universal mind. This philosophy does not place the individual at the center of the music, but rather, the world around him.

Collective Musical Unconsciousness

Many who believe in a collective musical unconsciousness contend that as we come into contact with others, we absorb or internalize a great deal of information. We take this data, filter it through our mind and soul, transform it someway, and then release it back into the world. It's a big merry-go-round of information. Others, who have a more traditional (Jungian) mindset, may contend that this collective unconsciousness is imprinted upon us through the very evolutionary process.

The main idea here is that musical thoughts are shared. They are communal property. The musician is only the temporary host. Musical ideas refract through us constantly but we do not own them. Instead, there is a kind of "group memory" that we harness.

Because of this, you could say that music's seed does not grow from the inside out, but rather, from the outside in. It is byproduct of the interrelatedness of all things. It is the result of wide-ranging interaction.

If you subscribe to this philosophy, you might contend that the musician acts as a medium between an audience and some collective spirit. When this happens, the music reveals itself to the player or the composer, not the other way around.

Music from Within

Others believe, quite oppositely, that music is the result of a very personal, exclusive, and even isolated, inward journey. They believe that music is the result of a desire, even need, to create order out of internal chaos. When thinking about music this way, you could say that the musician looks inside himself for clues on how to write a song, play a solo, and so on. He or she does not tap into some greater collective power, or "psychic inheritance."

This is not to say that this type of musician is detached from the outside world. Everybody has influences. However, the music created is the result of self-examination; it is independent, individualistic, and self-possessed. There also is no clear channeling of ideas from one person to another, or from generation to generation.

Some musicians conveniently pick and choose from both philosophies or even find a way to combine them. Others never even give it much thought; they do what they do and that's that. Whatever you believe, know that creating music is the result of both the intellect and the spirit.

Your intellect allows you to analyze music and to develop needed skills. Your soul, or spirit, allows you to emotionally respond to music. Your spirit is probably also what drove you to play music in the first place.

Seeking Balance

Finding a good balance between your mind and soul is vital. Some people will say that you should just feel the music when you play. This isn't totally true. When you perform, there are intellectual decisions that need to be made. You cannot and should not turn your mind off in the heat of the moment.

On the other hand, those who create music intended only to elicit an intellectual or analytical response usually create abysmal, boring music. This kind of music may look great on paper, or be interesting to study, but it lacks emotion and usually excitement.

After a practice session or a performance evaluate your success rate. To do this you will need to use your intellect. When performing, try to let the music flow from you organically. If you overthink, you'll kill the music.

When your intellect and spirit work together, you are using the full range of your faculties. Sometimes, you need to think through a problematic musical situation. Other times, your brain gets in the way and you need to just use your instincts. It's impossible for someone else to tell you when to use your intellect and when to use your instincts; this is up to you. However, it's best not to be too one-sided in your approach to music, or life for that matter.

Keep It Real and Natural

Don't use a performance situation to practice your favorite licks. Instead, let the music pour out naturally and try to contribute to the emotional energy of each tune. You never want to play clinically or in a transcriptional manner.

On the other hand, keep your wits about you in a performance situation. In between songs you may have a moment to reflect intellectually on your playing. But beware that overthinking may make your performance tentative or shy. There is an old saying, "If you make a mistake, make it loudly."

Enjoying Every Note You Play

If you're like most musicians, you will feel good about some performances and practice sessions but disappointed with others. The key is to not give in to musical depression. In fact, don't even accept ambivalence. Given the right attitude, you can enjoy every note you play.

Always Play Your Best

Sometimes a gig, rehearsal, or practice session may be going downright rotten. However, don't play judge and jury and hang yourself midway through the session. Play every note like you really mean it. Don't get lazy or cynical. Always play your best. If you feel disappointed at the end of the day, let it go. Get on with the now and maintain your faith in tomorrow. You can't change the past but you can learn from it.

If you decide that playing the drums is not for you, that's okay. Just don't come to this conclusion through pessimism. It should be the result of a thoughtful decision to pursue other interests.

Here are some other rules of thumb: Never degrade yourself in front of others, accept compliments, and, above all else, make sure your self-criticism is productive. You will only get worse by slinging insults at yourself.

Accepting Criticism

If others criticize you, hear them out. Try to learn from their insights. Don't take it personally, even if somebody is coming on a little strong. Understand that 99 percent of the criticism you will hear will be directed toward your current or most recent performance(s), not your overall abilities and potential. Finally, always remember that every person has the ability to make improvements, so take criticism in stride.

If you're disappointed in your work, be careful of your internal dialogue. Instead of saying "That was awful," say "I will do better next time." If you make a mistake, admit fault. Accept your musical responsibilities. However, never turn on yourself. Many musicians end up being their own worst enemies.

Realistic Outlooks

You will also enjoy playing more if you have a realistic outlook. Most musicians never get rich and famous. Most musicians never see their name in lights on a marquee.

Music should enhance your life. If you find that it doesn't, think about why. If it's because you're a ruthless self-critic, or you have unrealistic goals, you will probably never fully enjoy the gifts music has to offer. On the other hand, if you take your progress one day at a time and maintain a positive attitude, you will find that music is quite rewarding.

Vanity and materialism shouldn't be the impetus behind your decision to play the drums. Music making should be about personal enrichment. If you make some money along the way or if you become fortunate enough to make a living playing drums, wonderful. But don't expect to move mountains. Just enjoy playing and take pleasure in the fraternity music brings. If you have a "pie in the sky" attitude, you may soon find yourself very frustrated and unhappy. Ⓔ

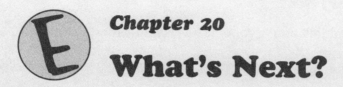

Chapter 20

What's Next?

In this final chapter, we'll discuss how to continue your musical education. So far, we've talked about critiquing your own playing, but we haven't directly addressed how to do this. We'll also explore the pros and cons of private instruction and talk about playing in a band. We'll round out the chapter with some closing information on self-improvement.

Continuing Your Education

If you've gotten this far in this book, chances are, you're on your way toward becoming a fine drummer. Hopefully, *The Everything® Drums Book* has laid the groundwork for your musical education.

What You've Learned

If you've used this book properly, you have learned a good deal about:

- Equipment
- Music reading
- Technique
- Musical styles
- Musical philosophy

Recognize, however, that there is still a great deal to learn. We have really just scratched the surface. Each and every chapter in this guide could be expanded into its own book. For this reason, it is important that you look through the appendices to decide where you need to go next. If it's a book worth buying, it's probably listed in Appendix B.

The world of music is vast and it takes a lifetime to explore even one style. No matter how proficient you become, there is still something new to learn. Your musical education will only end when you decide you've had enough. If you're serious about music, this will be when you grow old and tire. Some pursue their education until the day they die.

Learning an instrument is not like learning how to ride a bicycle recreationally. You can buy a bike and learn how to balance on two wheels in a matter of days, maybe even hours. From that day forward, you've got it licked. You're done.

Music does not work this way at all. With music, even that which you've already learned gets rusty unless you review it constantly. And it doesn't stop there. There's always more than can be done to refine your technique, sharpen your reading skills, help you to play grooves and fills more idiomatically, or to solo more creatively.

So the question you should ask yourself is "Where do I go from here?" In Chapter 1, you were asked to make a list of your personal goals. You were advised to review this list weekly, make revisions, and then reflect on how your goals may have changed over time. If you've been doing this, you should have a pretty good idea of your strengths and weaknesses by now. You should also be more informed about music on the whole. Given this, it should be easier to set realistic goals and follow through with them.

QUESTION?

What music style should I pursue?
Out of all the exercises in this book, think about what style of music you enjoyed playing the most. Your answer should point you in the right direction.

How to Critique Your Playing

We've talked a lot about critiquing your own playing and advice on how to do so is scattered throughout the book. However, we need to take a moment to put all of this into perspective.

You know now that when you practice, it's not enough just to play. It's important to be organized in your approach and to plan ahead of time. You also need to infuse your music with both mind and spirit. Lastly, you should be turning into quite a self-adjudicator by now.

Let's review some types of questions you should ask yourself each day you practice. Start by asking yourself:

- What did I practice yesterday?
- Did I accomplish this task?
- Am I satisfied with my progress?
- Do I need to go back and review or am I ready to move on to something else?

If you feel that you're ready to move on in your studies, ask yourself these questions:

- What is the next logical step?
- What needs focusing on?

- What are my ultimate goals?
- Am I working gradually but steadily toward meeting these goals or have I strayed?

If you've been performing with others, reflect on your most recent experiences. Ask yourself the following questions:

- How successful was my performance?
- What sounded good?
- What needs improvement?
- How should I structure my practice time to make these improvements?
- Was there any constructive criticism given to me? If so, what?
- Do I agree with this criticism? If not, why?
- In general, was I well received by the other musicians? If not, why?
- What can I do to make my playing better the next time I perform?

Strong critical-thinking skills make for strong performances. Teach yourself to think about, and keep track of, everything you've done leading up to your performance. Then, when the time comes, it'll all come out naturally.

Asking questions, and finding pragmatic solutions, is very important. This is how you assess your skill level and better understand your needs and goals. This doesn't mean that you grill yourself day in and day out. These questions should come naturally; you needn't interrogate yourself. Through gentle self-analysis, your playing will improve on its own.

The Pros and Cons of Private Instruction

Taking private lessons is highly recommended. In fact, you may even want to review the exercises in this book with a teacher. Even if you've followed the instruction in this book to the letter, chances are you've still developed a bad habit along the way or misinterpreted something.

It's not easy to be an impartial judge when it's you you're evaluating. One of the most difficult things to do is to step outside of your body and critique yourself. Your perception is always biased one way or another. This is where a teacher comes into the picture.

Why You Should Take Lessons

Every drummer should take at least a handful of lessons. If you're serious about playing the drums, it's recommended that you find a qualified teacher and work under her or his tutelage for years. As you become more advanced, you should study with a variety of teachers. To do this, it sometimes requires travel to different cities, states (or provinces), or even countries. Even professional drummers take lessons from time to time.

You may be surprised to know that such topnotch professionals as Neil Peart, Steve Smith, Dave Weckl, Danny Gottlieb, Max Weinberg, and others have all taken lessons, well into their professional years. Educational guru and master drummer Joe Morello once said that if his teacher George Lawrence Stone was still alive, he'd still be taking lessons. Morello has been a first-rate jazz drummer since the 1950s and is probably the best living snare drummer.

If Joe Morello still confesses the need to improve, what does this tell you about your playing? It should tell you to always remain a student. It's arrogant to think that you don't need lessons or that you already know everything.

Self-taught musicians sometimes say they don't want to take lessons because they think a teacher will somehow spoil their individuality or take away their creative spirit. This is complete hogwash. These types of players are usually misguided, insecure, lazy, or all of the above.

When working with any teacher, you may find that there are some things you reject. This is okay, as long as you don't do it out of ignorance. If you find that you disagree with your teacher constantly, then you've selected the wrong teacher; move on. But to categorically reject private instruction for fear of losing your uniqueness is silly.

Music is best learned through apprenticeship, because it is a skill as well as an art form. When working with a teacher, you will have someone to bounce ideas off of and someone to share in your triumphs and defeats. Most of all, you will also have a reliable personal critic. Learning to play any instrument is hard. Why not let someone help you? It will make the journey a lot less bumpy.

The Downside

Is there a downside to private instruction? The only way a teacher can harm your playing is if you select somebody who's unqualified. Incompetent teachers are out there, so beware. The scary thing is, many of these teachers don't even realize they're inept. A lot of musicians talk a good game, too, but can't deliver. So you have to be careful in your selection.

Questions You Should Ask

Following is a list of questions to ask a prospective teacher followed by some commentary on each item.

What do you charge?

A quality teacher usually charges the going rate around town. Very successful instructors may charge even a little more, since their talents command it. Inept teachers may offer lower prices just to entice you.

How long will each lesson be?

Depending on your degree of seriousness and your age, you should take a half-hour or hour lesson. Some teachers also offer forty-five minute slots. A good teacher is also usually not opposed to giving you a little overtime if necessary.

What will I need to bring to each lesson?

Quality teachers will tell you to bring your sticks, whatever books they ask you to purchase, and a notebook of some kind. They also may advise you to bring a tape recorder to each lesson. The notebook is used to write down each week's assignments and to write out nonpublished exercises, beats, fills, and so on.

Will my lessons be weekly?

A quality teacher will usually assume that you want a weekly lesson, and will be very happy to find a suitable day and time for you. However, some teachers can be overly loose about scheduling. If they hem and haw and can't nail down a specific day and time for your weekly lesson, find a different teacher.

What's your cancellation and rescheduling policy?

Teachers get taken advantage of constantly. They often deal with students who have spotty attendance or are consistently tardy. Because of this, most good teachers have strict policies concerning cancellation and rescheduling. Some teachers even make their students or students' parents sign a contract stating that if a lesson is missed, it will be paid for anyway. Exceptions are typically made for bad weather, family emergencies, or illness. If a lesson *is* missed, teachers usually ask for twenty-four hour notice.

If you take lessons, be sensitive to the needs of the teacher. If you don't show up for your lesson, they lose money, and can't put food on their table. For most, teaching isn't their hobby, it's their livelihood. And unlike their counterparts in public schools, private instructors don't have a union to support them, or another paycheck coming in from a district office somewhere.

Because of this, it's important that you keep your appointments. If you forget about a lesson, it's customary to pay anyway. You're reserving the teacher's time each week whether you're there or not.

Following are some additional questions to ask a prospective teacher:

What do you expect of me each week?

A good teacher will say to practice *at least* a half an hour per day and to maintain regular attendance.

What's your educational background?

A good teacher usually has a bachelor's degree in music from a reputable college. Many of them even have a master's or doctorate degree. However, some teachers are schooled in another way. You may come across a teacher who has gained a great deal of real-life experience but does not have an academic degree. These teachers can also be quite helpful, and in some cases, even more pragmatic in their assignments. Either way, you want a teacher who really knows his or her subject matter. You also want a teacher who has good communication skills.

What aspects of drumming do you concentrate on with your students?

A good teacher should mention the big four: technique, reading, styles, and philosophy. A good teacher should also be interested in addressing your individual needs and concerns.

Are you a performing musician?

Some teachers only teach. They don't perform themselves. Often this is true with school music teachers. For school music teachers this is not desirable but is acceptable since their job is really to inspire kids, get them started on an instrument, and to teach fundamentals. If a student is particularly talented, a responsible schoolteacher will seek out suitable private instruction. School music teachers are generalists by nature. Private instructors need to be qualified specialists.

Given this, private instructors need to have extensive performing experience. Unfortunately not all of them do. These kinds of private instructors fall into the George Bernard Shaw category. Shaw wrote, "Those who can do. Those who cannot, teach." This is a cynical dig against teachers, but in some cases, it resonates truthfully.

ESSENTIAL

You want a teacher who is a working musician; you want a teacher who is out there interacting in the field. Those who don't perform are often ignorant about what it takes to really be a musician. So make sure you study with somebody who can teach you not just book knowledge, but lessons from the school of hard knocks.

Straight Talk about Joining a Band

Playing in a band is an essential rite of passage for any musician. It's not very hard to meet musicians. They're everywhere. All you have to do is start hitting some jam sessions or live music clubs. Soon, you find yourself in the company of musicians who enjoy the same music that you do.

Starting a band is pretty painless. However, finding suitable work for a band is not always so easy, especially if you have vaulting ambitions or want to make a living through music. If you're just in it to have fun, you will have a smoother road ahead. On the other hand, if you're looking for public adoration or hefty royalty checks, you will have to be pretty resilient. No matter what your goals, the payoff is great even though you will suffer disappointment from time to time.

When you have a close-knit group, it feels a bit like having a second family. Not only are you working with others toward a common goal, you just might develop some of the most meaningful relationships of your life. The downside is that the honeymoon doesn't last forever. Sometimes friendships splinter as musical interests change or personal problems take center stage. Other times, money becomes an issue, as it can be expensive to finance a band.

In the end, is it worth playing in a band versus just freelancing? Absolutely it is. If you love music, playing on a stage with other like-minded musicians is downright electrifying.

However, regardless of the band's collective needs, make sure that you keep your musical needs at the forefront. This does not mean that you should be selfish. This simply means to enjoy whatever you play. If your band starts to move in a direction that doesn't suit you, rather than being bored or discontented, move on to another project. Play only in bands that bring you joy, and work only with the musicians who enrich your life.

Freelancing

Good freelance musicians are like chameleons, because they know how to fit in with just about any musical surrounding. If you want to freelance, you will need to know how to play just about every musical style. You will also need to be able to learn tunes quickly and have quick musical reflexes. Often, freelancers will enter into a musical situation and be expected to perform at a high level with no rehearsal. Also, as a freelancer, chances are you will be working with unfamiliar faces on each gig or recording session. This requires that you have the ability to adapt well to other players' approaches.

Above all else, keep a sense of humor about you. The music industry can be unreliable and horribly unpredictable at times. The better you're able to adapt and laugh things off, the further you will go.

If you choose to become a freelancer, you will need to be able to read music well. You will also need to be able to play virtually every genre of music, including a wide range of ethnic styles. In addition, you will need to be a good listener and be able to acclimate quickly to a multiplicity of situations. Further, you will need to be able to follow musicians' hand signals well. Finally, you will also need to maintain a positive and agreeable attitude on gigs; otherwise, you won't be hired back. Moreover, freelancers should maintain a conservative appearance. You won't get freelancing work if you have five nose rings and green hair.

If you become a freelancer, you will meet a wide assortment of people in your travels, and your musical perspective will probably broaden as the years go by. If you're good, you will also probably work more, and make more money than someone who plays in only one band.

Musically speaking, the downside of freelancing is that you may never become truly great at any single style of music. Since freelancing means that you focus on becoming a musical generalist, you may never really excel at any one genre. Freelancers tend to be very good at a little bit of everything, but not groundbreaking in any one specific area.

There is a downside to becoming a specialist, too. If you chose this road, you may become a one-dance pony or your musical viewpoint may grow narrow.

Either way you go, there are tradeoffs to be made. It's best to find some balance, but most of all, try to find your own niche where you will be musically happy.

Being Better Than You Were Yesterday

The music business is very competitive. A little competitiveness is healthy. However, a lot of it can be harmful, because competition tends to interfere with personal enrichment. If you feel like you always have to be better than everybody else, you're setting the bar too high. How about just being better than *you* were yesterday? Don't compulsively compare yourself to other drummers. You're bound either to develop a false sense of grandeur or feel that your playing is totally inadequate. Both attitudes will interfere in your progress.

The more you feed your ego, the more you will probably falter. Perfectionism, for example, is a big problem with musicians. Somewhere along the way, some players learned that they had to play impeccably all the time. True, top pros rarely make egregious errors in public. But they also know how to cover up their mistakes. They know how to make great saves; their recoveries are usually seamless and undetectable.

Keep Your Goals Clear

Don't pursue perfection; pursue truth and excellence in music. Your drumming will have a lot more soul if you do this. Also, by doing this, your blunders will be naturally reduced. If you set your sights on perfection, you will probably do the opposite. Why? You will stumble because you're expecting the impossible. Perfectionism is unattainable. End of story.

Stay Relaxed

On the other hand, your playing will improve when you learn to relax onstage, give it your all, and not fret relentlessly over mistakes. If your internal dialogue is on endless loop saying "Don't screw up . . . You can't screw up . . . Play perfectly . . . Impress the leader . . . ," guess what will probably happen? You'll bomb. Instead of trying to prove that you're the best drummer in town or the best drummer in the whole wide world, try just being better than you were yesterday. By doing this, you will shift your focus toward something concrete and attainable.

A Final Note

Let's cap off this book with a brief but true story:

There was once an old man playing drums in a Dixieland band in a little outdoor café in New Orleans. It was a sweltering day but the band was really swinging. A precocious young boy came up to the man on the break and asked him what he should do to be a great drummer. The man just grinned and said, "Here," and handed his sticks to the little boy. "Don't ever take these sticks out of your hands." The boy gazed down at the sticks in amazement as the old man walked off.

It's really that simple. To become a solid, competent player you need to keep those sticks in your hands. Good luck and enjoy the journey.

Appendices

Appendix A

Drummer Discography

Appendix B

Resources

Appendix A

Drummer Discography

Following is a list of celebrated drummers together with one or two album recommendations. Unless stated otherwise, the recordings listed are albums by the drummers themselves. There are many other important drummers, who, for lack of space, have not been included here. However, this list should serve as a good starting point when learning about the rich history of drumming.

Rock and Pop Drummers

Kenny Aronoff: *The Lonesome Jubilee* (John Mellencamp)

Carter Beauford: *Crash* and *Live in Chicago* (both with Dave Matthews)

Hal Blaine: *Help Me Rhonda* (the Beach Boys) and *Bridge Over Troubled Water* (Simon and Garfunkel)

John Bonham: *Led Zeppelin II Led Zeppelin III* (both with Led Zeppelin)

Matt Cameron: *Badmotorfinger* (Soundgarden)

Stewart Copeland: *Zenyatta Mondatta* and *Ghost in the Machine* (both with the Police)

Peter Criss: *Alive!* (Kiss)

John Densmore: *The Doors* and *Absolutely Live* (both with the Doors)

D. J. Fontana: *Heartbreak Hotel* and *Hound Dog* (both with Elvis Presley)

Dave Grohl: *Nevermind* (Nirvana)

Levon Helm: *Music from Big Pink* (the Band)

Manu Katché: *Nothing Like the Sun* (Sting) and *So* (Peter Gabriel)

Russ Kunkle: *Running on Empty* (Jackson Browne)

Nick Mason: *Dark Side of the Moon* and *The Wall* (both with Pink Floyd)

Mitch Mitchell: *Are You Experienced?* (Jimi Hendrix)

Keith Moon: *The Who Sings My Generation* and *Tommy* (both with the Who)

Larry Mullen, Jr.: *The Joshua Tree* and *Rattle and Hum* (both with U2)

Ian Paice: *The Book of Taliesyn* (Deep Purple)

Neil Peart: *2112* and *Test For Echo* (both with Rush)

Mike Portnoy: *Six Degrees of Inner Turbulence* (Dream Theater)

Phil Selway: *OK Computer* (Radiohead)

Chad Smith: *Blood Sugar Sex Magik* and *One Hot Minute* (Red Hot Chili Peppers)

Ringo Starr: *Help* and *Abbey Road* (both with the Beatles)

Alex Van Halen: *Diver Down* and *1984* (both with Van Halen)

Max Weinberg: *Born to Run* (Bruce Springsteen)

Alan White: *Tales from Topographic Oceans* (Yes) and *Imagine* (John Lennon)

Swing and Big Band Drummers

Louie Bellson: *Thunderbird* and *West Coast Party* (the latter with Duke Ellington)

Big Sid Catlett: *Louis Armstrong and the All-Stars* (Louis Armstrong)

Cozy Cole: *Topsy*

Jo Jones: *The Essential Jo Jones* and *Prez at His Very Best* (the latter with Lester Young)

Gene Krupa: *Uptown* and *Live at Carnegie Hall* (the latter with Benny Goodman)

Mel Lewis: *Mel Lewis and the Jazz Orchestra* and *Consummation (*both co-lead with Thad Jones)

Buddy Rich: *Big Swing Face* and *The Monster*

Dave Tough: *His First Herd* and *The Thundering Herd* (both with Woody Herman)

Chick Webb: *A Legend Vol. 1* and *King of the Savoy Vol. 2*

Bebop and Contemporary Jazz

Art Blakey: *Moanin'* and *A Night in Tunisia*

Terry Lyne Carrington: *I Remember* (Dianne Reeves) and *Joy Rider* (Wayne Shorter)

Kenny Clarke: *La Rondo* (Modern Jazz Quartet) and *The Giant* (Dizzy Gillespie)

Jimmy Cobb: *Kind of Blue* (Miles Davis) and *Full House* (Wes Montgomery)

Jack DeJohnette: *Special Edition* and *Parallel Realities*

Peter Erskine: *As It Is* and *Invitation* (the latter with Jaco Pastorius)

Roy Haynes: *We Three* and *In Action* (The latter with Thelonious Monk)

Elvin Jones: *Elvin!* and *A Love Supreme* (the latter with John Coltrane)

Philly Joe Jones: *Everybody Digs Bill Evans* (Bill Evans) and *Milestones* (Miles Davis)

Shelly Manne: *Manne Kind* and *Empathy* (the latter with Bill Evans)

Joe Morello: *Time Out* and *Live at Carnegie Hall* (both with Dave Brubeck)

Paul Motian: *Sunday at the Village Vanguard* (Bill Evans)

Max Roach: *Freedom Now Suite* and *Live at Basin Street* (the latter with Clifford Brown)

Ed Thigpen: *Affinity* and *We Get Requests* (both with Oscar Peterson)

Jeff Watts: *Citizen Tain* and *Trio Jeepy* (the latter with Branford Marsalis)

Paul Wertico: *First Circle* and *Still Life (Talking)* (Pat Metheny)

Tony Williams: *Lifetime* and *Miles Smiles* (the latter with Miles Davis)

Latin Drum Set Players

Robert Ameen: *New Faces* (Dizzy Gillespie)

Horacio "El Negro" Hernandez: *Triangulo* (Michel Camillo)

Walfredo Reyes, Jr.: *The Road* (Luis Conte) and *Speed of Light* (Flora Purim)

Antonio Sanchez: *Speaking of Now* (Pat Metheny) and *Motherland* (Danilo Perez)

Michael Shrieve: *Woodstock* (Carlos Santana)

Crossgenre Drummers

Ginger Baker: *Going Back Home* and *Live at the Fillmore* (the latter with Cream)

Cyndi Blackman: *In the Now* (Cyndi also performs live with Lenny Kravitz.)

Terry Bozzio: *Solos and Duets Vols. 1 and 2* (co-lead with drummer Chad Wackerman) and *Rhyme and Reason* (Missing Persons)

Bill Bruford: *Fragile* (Yes) and *The Sound of Surprise* (Earthworks)

Dennis Chambers: *Alive in America* (Steely Dan) and *Tokyo Live* (John McLaughlin)

Billy Cobham: *Spectrum* and *Skydive* (the latter with Freddie Hubbard)

Vinnie Colaiuta: *Joe's Garage* (Frank Zappa) and *Ten Summoner's Tales* (Sting)

Phil Collins: *A Hot Night in Paris* and *Selling England by the Pound* (the latter with Genesis)

Steve Gadd: *Leprechaun* (Chick Corea) and *Still Crazy After All These Years* (Paul Simon)

Danny Gottlieb: *Watercolors* (Pat Metheny) and *Forward Motion* (Mark Egan)

Mickey Hart: *Diga* (Diga Rhythm Band) and *Terrapin Station* (the Grateful Dead)

Jim Keltner: *Journeyman* (Eric Clapton) and *There Is Always One More Time* (B. B. King)

Earl Palmer: *Unforgettable* (Dinah Washington) and *Georgia Peach* (Little Richard)

Jeff Porcaro: *Gaucho* (Steely Dan) and *Toto* (Toto)

Steve Smith: *Frontiers* (Journey) and *Global Beat* (Vital Information)

Charlie Watts: *A Tribute to Charlie Parker with Strings* and *Voodoo Lounge* (the latter with the Rolling Stones)

Dave Weckl: *Rhythm of the Soul* and *The Elektrik Band* (the latter with Chick Corea)

Appendix B

Resources

Beginner to Intermediate Snare Drum Methods

Alfred's Drum Method: Book I and Book II, by Sandy Feldstein and Dave Black; Alfred Publishing Co., 1987.

A Fresh Approach to the Snare Drum, by Mark Wessels; Mark Wessels Publications, 1994.

Podemski's Standard Snare Drum Method, by Benjamin Podemski; Columbia Pictures Publications, 1986.

Systematic Approach for the Developing Snare Drummer, by John A. Fatta; Beatnik Publishing, 2002.

Intermediate to Advanced Snare Drum Studies

America's N.A.R.D. Drum Solos, by Frank Arsenault, et al.; Ludwig Publications, 1962.

Master Studies, by Joe Morello; Modern Drummer Publications, 1995.

Modern Rudimental Swing Solos for the Advanced Drummer, by Charles S. Wilcoxin; Ludwig Music, Inc., 1941.

Modern School for Snare Drum, by Morris Goldenberg; Warner Brothers Publications, 2002.

Portraits in Rhythm, by Anthony Cirone; Warner Brothers Publications, 1999.

Stick Control for the Snare Drummer and *Accents and Rebounds,* by George L. Stone; George B. Stone & Son Publishing, 1998.

Concept Books

4-Way Coordination, by Marvin Dahlgren and Elliot Fine; Warner Brothers Publications, 2000.

Inside Buddy Rich, by Buddy Rich and Jim Nesbitt; Kendor Music, 1984.

The New Breed and *The New Breed II,* by Gary Chester; Hal Leonard Publishing, 1986 and 1990.

Syncopation for the Modern Drummer, by Ted Reed; Alfred Publishing Co., 1997.

When in Doubt, Roll!, by Bill Bruford; Hal Leonard Publishing, 1988.

Rock and Funk Books

The Drummer's Cookbook by John Pickering; Mel Bay Publications, 1993.

Future Sounds by David Garibaldi; Alfred Music Publishing, 1993.

Groovezilla Drum Method, by Kevin Soltis and Jim Linsner; Rhythm Methods Publications, 1999.

Play Rock Drums, by Joel Rothman; Amsco Music, 1999.

Updated Realistic Rock, by Carmine Appice; Warner Brothers Publications, 2000.

Afro-Latin Books

Afro-Cuban Rhythms for Drumset, by Frank Malabe and Bob Weiner; Warner Brothers Publications, 1994.

Practical Applications: Using Afro-Caribbean Rhythms, Parts 1, 2, and 3, by Chuck Silverman; Warner Brothers Publications, 2000.

West African Rhythms for Drumset, by Royal Hartigan with Abraham Adzenyah and Freeman Donkor; Warner Brothers Publications, 1995.

Jazz Books

Advanced Techniques for the Modern Drummer, by Jim Chapin; Warner Brothers Publications, 2002.

The Art of Bop Drumming and *Beyond Bop Drumming,* by John Riley; Warner Brothers Publications, 1994 and 1997.

The Art of Modern Jazz Drumming, by Jack DeJohnette and Charlie Perry; D.C. Publications, 1984.

Standard Time: Jazz Drums, by Steve Davis; Jamey Aebersold Jazz, Inc., 1994.

Miscellaneous

Bass Drum Control Solos, by Colin Bailey; Hal Leonard Publishing, 2002.

The Cymbal Book, by Hugo Pinksterboer; Hal Leonard Publishing, 1993.

The Drum Set Soloist, by Steve Houghton; Warner Brothers Publications, 1996.

Even in the Odds, by Ralph Humphrey; C.L. Barnhouse Publications.

The Sound of Brushes, by Ed Thigpen; Warner Brothers Publications, 2000.

Videos

Everything Is Timekeeping, by Peter Erskine; DCI Music Video.

Legends of Jazz Drumming, Parts 1 and 2; DCI Music Video.

The Living Art of Brushes, by Clayton Cameron; DCI Music Video.

The Natural Approach to Technique, by Joe Morello; Hot Licks Productions.

A Work in Progress, by Neil Peart; DCI Music Video, 1996.

Web Sites

✍ *www.chucksilverman.com:* lots of advice on Latin drumming and rudiments

✍ *www.drumbum.com:* lots of helpful advice on drumming styles and technique

✍ *www.drumlink.com:* an informative drum magazine called *Drum!*

✍ *www.drummingweb.com:* information about technique, styles, reading notation, etc.

✍ *www.drumplace.com:* information on all aspects of drumming

✍ *www.drumweb.com:* information about retailers, manufacturers, and famous drummers

✍ *www.foreverdrumming.com:* a resource for instructional books and videos

✍ *www.moderndrummer.com: Modern Drummer* is the best and most widely read drum magazine available

✍ *www.musicbooksplus.com:* a resource for instructional books and videos

✍ *www.pas.org:* Percussive Arts Society's Web site

✍ *www.stickitonline.com:* an informative drum magazine called *Stick It!*

Index

THE EVERYTHING SERIES!

BUSINESS

Everything® **Business Planning Book**
Everything® **Coaching and Mentoring Book**
Everything® **Fundraising Book**
Everything® **Home-Based Business Book**
Everything® **Leadership Book**
Everything® **Managing People Book**
Everything® **Network Marketing Book**
Everything® **Online Business Book**
Everything® **Project Management Book**
Everything® **Selling Book**
Everything® **Start Your Own Business Book**
Everything® **Time Management Book**

COMPUTERS

Everything® **Build Your Own Home Page Book**
Everything® **Computer Book**
Everything® **Internet Book**
Everything® **Microsoft® Word 2000 Book**

COOKBOOKS

Everything® **Barbecue Cookbook**
Everything® **Bartender's Book, $9.95**
Everything® **Chinese Cookbook**
Everything® **Chocolate Cookbook**
Everything® **Cookbook**
Everything® **Dessert Cookbook**
Everything® **Diabetes Cookbook**
Everything® **Indian Cookbook**
Everything® **Low-Carb Cookbook**
Everything® **Low-Fat High-Flavor Cookbook**

Everything® **Low-Salt Cookbook**
Everything® **Mediterranean Cookbook**
Everything® **Mexican Cookbook**
Everything® **One-Pot Cookbook**
Everything® **Pasta Book**
Everything® **Quick Meals Cookbook**
Everything® **Slow Cooker Cookbook**
Everything® **Soup Cookbook**
Everything® **Thai Cookbook**
Everything® **Vegetarian Cookbook**
Everything® **Wine Book**

HEALTH

Everything® **Alzheimer's Book**
Everything® **Anti-Aging Book**
Everything® **Diabetes Book**
Everything® **Dieting Book**
Everything® **Herbal Remedies Book**
Everything® **Hypnosis Book**
Everything® **Massage Book**
Everything® **Menopause Book**
Everything® **Nutrition Book**
Everything® **Reflexology Book**
Everything® **Reiki Book**
Everything® **Stress Management Book**
Everything® **Vitamins, Minerals, and Nutritional Supplements Book**

HISTORY

Everything® **American Government Book**
Everything® **American History Book**
Everything® **Civil War Book**
Everything® **Irish History & Heritage Book**

Everything® **Mafia Book**
Everything® **Middle East Book**
Everything® **World War II Book**

HOBBIES & GAMES

Everything® **Bridge Book**
Everything® **Candlemaking Book**
Everything® **Casino Gambling Book**
Everything® **Chess Basics Book**
Everything® **Collectibles Book**
Everything® **Crossword and Puzzle Book**
Everything® **Digital Photography Book**
Everything® **Easy Crosswords Book**
Everything® **Family Tree Book**
Everything® **Games Book**
Everything® **Knitting Book**
Everything® **Magic Book**
Everything® **Motorcycle Book**
Everything® **Online Genealogy Book**
Everything® **Photography Book**
Everything® **Pool & Billiards Book**
Everything® **Quilting Book**
Everything® **Scrapbooking Book**
Everything® **Sewing Book**
Everything® **Soapmaking Book**

HOME IMPROVEMENT

Everything® **Feng Shui Book**
Everything® **Feng Shui Decluttering Book, $9.95 ($15.95 CAN)**
Everything® **Fix-It Book**
Everything® **Gardening Book**
Everything® **Homebuilding Book**

All Everything® books are priced at $12.95 or $14.95, unless otherwise stated. Prices subject to change without notice.
Canadian prices range from $11.95–$31.95, and are subject to change without notice.

Everything® **Home Decorating Book**
Everything® **Landscaping Book**
Everything® **Lawn Care Book**
Everything® **Organize Your Home Book**

EVERYTHING® KIDS' BOOKS

All titles are $6.95
Everything® **Kids' Baseball Book, 3rd Ed.** ($10.95 CAN)
Everything® **Kids' Bible Trivia Book** ($10.95 CAN)
Everything® **Kids' Bugs Book** ($10.95 CAN)
Everything® **Kids' Christmas Puzzle & Activity Book** ($10.95 CAN)
Everything® **Kids' Cookbook** ($10.95 CAN)
Everything® **Kids' Halloween Puzzle & Activity Book** ($10.95 CAN)
Everything® **Kids' Joke Book** ($10.95 CAN)
Everything® **Kids' Math Puzzles Book** ($10.95 CAN)
Everything® **Kids' Mazes Book** ($10.95 CAN)
Everything® **Kids' Money Book** ($11.95 CAN)
Everything® **Kids' Monsters Book** ($10.95 CAN)
Everything® **Kids' Nature Book** ($11.95 CAN)
Everything® **Kids' Puzzle Book** ($10.95 CAN)
Everything® **Kids' Riddles & Brain Teasers Book** ($10.95 CAN)
Everything® **Kids' Science Experiments Book** ($10.95 CAN)
Everything® **Kids' Soccer Book** ($10.95 CAN)
Everything® **Kids' Travel Activity Book** ($10.95 CAN)

KIDS' STORY BOOKS

Everything® **Bedtime Story Book**
Everything® **Bible Stories Book**
Everything® **Fairy Tales Book**
Everything® **Mother Goose Book**

LANGUAGE

Everything® **Inglés Book**
Everything® **Learning French Book**
Everything® **Learning German Book**
Everything® **Learning Italian Book**
Everything® **Learning Latin Book**
Everything® **Learning Spanish Book**
Everything® **Sign Language Book**
Everything® **Spanish Phrase Book, $9.95** ($15.95 CAN)

MUSIC

Everything® **Drums Book (with CD), $19.95** ($31.95 CAN)
Everything® **Guitar Book**
Everything® **Playing Piano and Keyboards Book**
Everything® **Rock & Blues Guitar Book (with CD), $19.95** ($31.95 CAN)
Everything® **Songwriting Book**

NEW AGE

Everything® **Astrology Book**
Everything® **Divining the Future Book**
Everything® **Dreams Book**
Everything® **Ghost Book**
Everything® **Love Signs Book, $9.95** ($15.95 CAN)
Everything® **Meditation Book**
Everything® **Numerology Book**
Everything® **Palmistry Book**
Everything® **Psychic Book**
Everything® **Spells & Charms Book**
Everything® **Tarot Book**
Everything® **Wicca and Witchcraft Book**

PARENTING

Everything® **Baby Names Book**
Everything® **Baby Shower Book**
Everything® **Baby's First Food Book**
Everything® **Baby's First Year Book**
Everything® **Breastfeeding Book**

Everything® **Father-to-Be Book**
Everything® **Get Ready for Baby Book**
Everything® **Getting Pregnant Book**
Everything® **Homeschooling Book**
Everything® **Parent's Guide to Children with Autism**
Everything® **Parent's Guide to Positive Discipline**
Everything® **Parent's Guide to Raising a Successful Child**
Everything® **Parenting a Teenager Book**
Everything® **Potty Training Book, $9.95** ($15.95 CAN)
Everything® **Pregnancy Book, 2nd Ed.**
Everything® **Pregnancy Fitness Book**
Everything® **Pregnancy Organizer, $15.00** ($22.95 CAN)
Everything® **Toddler Book**
Everything® **Tween Book**

PERSONAL FINANCE

Everything® **Budgeting Book**
Everything® **Get Out of Debt Book**
Everything® **Get Rich Book**
Everything® **Homebuying Book, 2nd Ed.**
Everything® **Homeselling Book**
Everything® **Investing Book**
Everything® **Money Book**
Everything® **Mutual Funds Book**
Everything® **Online Investing Book**
Everything® **Personal Finance Book**
Everything® **Personal Finance in Your 20s & 30s Book**
Everything® **Wills & Estate Planning Book**

PETS

Everything® **Cat Book**
Everything® **Dog Book**
Everything® **Dog Training and Tricks Book**
Everything® **Golden Retriever Book**
Everything® **Horse Book**
Everything® **Labrador Retriever Book**
Everything® **Puppy Book**
Everything® **Tropical Fish Book**

All Everything® books are priced at $12.95 or $14.95, unless otherwise stated. Prices subject to change without notice.
Canadian prices range from $11.95–$31.95, and are subject to change without notice.

REFERENCE

Everything® **Astronomy Book**
Everything® **Car Care Book**
Everything® **Christmas Book, $15.00**
($21.95 CAN)
Everything® **Classical Mythology Book**
Everything® **Einstein Book**
Everything® **Etiquette Book**
Everything® **Great Thinkers Book**
Everything® **Philosophy Book**
Everything® **Psychology Book**
Everything® **Shakespeare Book**
Everything® **Tall Tales, Legends, & Other Outrageous Lies Book**
Everything® **Toasts Book**
Everything® **Trivia Book**
Everything® **Weather Book**

RELIGION

Everything® **Angels Book**
Everything® **Bible Book**
Everything® **Buddhism Book**
Everything® **Catholicism Book**
Everything® **Christianity Book**
Everything® **Jewish History & Heritage Book**
Everything® **Judaism Book**
Everything® **Prayer Book**
Everything® **Saints Book**
Everything® **Understanding Islam Book**
Everything® **World's Religions Book**
Everything® **Zen Book**

SCHOOL & CAREERS

Everything® **After College Book**
Everything® **Alternative Careers Book**
Everything® **College Survival Book**
Everything® **Cover Letter Book**
Everything® **Get-a-Job Book**
Everything® **Hot Careers Book**

Everything® **Job Interview Book**
Everything® **New Teacher Book**
Everything® **Online Job Search Book**
Everything® **Resume Book, 2nd Ed.**
Everything® **Study Book**

SELF-HELP/ RELATIONSHIPS

Everything® **Dating Book**
Everything® **Divorce Book**
Everything® **Great Marriage Book**
Everything® **Great Sex Book**
Everything® **Kama Sutra Book**
Everything® **Romance Book**
Everything® **Self-Esteem Book**
Everything® **Success Book**

SPORTS & FITNESS

Everything® **Body Shaping Book**
Everything® **Fishing Book**
Everything® **Fly-Fishing Book**
Everything® **Golf Book**
Everything® **Golf Instruction Book**
Everything® **Knots Book**
Everything® **Pilates Book**
Everything® **Running Book**
Everything® **Sailing Book, 2nd Ed.**
Everything® **T'ai Chi and QiGong Book**
Everything® **Total Fitness Book**
Everything® **Weight Training Book**
Everything® **Yoga Book**

TRAVEL

Everything® **Family Guide to Hawaii**
Everything® **Guide to Las Vegas**
Everything® **Guide to New England**
Everything® **Guide to New York City**
Everything® **Guide to Washington D.C.**
Everything® **Travel Guide to The Disneyland Resort®, California Adventure®,**

Universal Studios®, and the Anaheim Area
Everything® **Travel Guide to the Walt Disney World Resort®, Universal Studios®, and Greater Orlando, 3rd Ed.**

WEDDINGS

Everything® **Bachelorette Party Book, $9.95** ($15.95 CAN)
Everything® **Bridesmaid Book, $9.95** ($15.95 CAN)
Everything® **Creative Wedding Ideas Book**
Everything® **Elopement Book, $9.95** ($15.95 CAN)
Everything® **Groom Book**
Everything® **Jewish Wedding Book**
Everything® **Wedding Book, 2nd Ed.**
Everything® **Wedding Checklist, $7.95** ($11.95 CAN)
Everything® **Wedding Etiquette Book, $7.95** ($11.95 CAN)
Everything® **Wedding Organizer, $15.00** ($22.95 CAN)
Everything® **Wedding Shower Book, $7.95** ($12.95 CAN)
Everything® **Wedding Vows Book, $7.95** ($11.95 CAN)
Everything® **Weddings on a Budget Book, $9.95** ($15.95 CAN)

WRITING

Everything® **Creative Writing Book**
Everything® **Get Published Book**
Everything® **Grammar and Style Book**
Everything® **Grant Writing Book**
Everything® **Guide to Writing Children's Books**
Everything® **Screenwriting Book**
Everything® **Writing Well Book**

Available wherever books are sold!
To order, call 800-872-5627, or visit us at everything.com

Everything® and everything.com® are registered trademarks of F+W Publications, Inc.

Software License Agreement

YOU SHOULD CAREFULLY READ THE FOLLOWING TERMS AND CONDITIONS BEFORE USING THIS SOFTWARE PRODUCT. INSTALLING AND USING THIS PRODUCT INDICATES YOUR ACCEPTANCE OF THESE CONDITIONS. IF YOU DO NOT AGREE WITH THESE TERMS AND CONDITIONS, DO NOT INSTALL THE SOFTWARE AND RETURN THIS PACKAGE PROMPTLY FOR A FULL REFUND.

1. Grant of License

This software package is protected under United States copyright law and international treaty. You are hereby entitled to one copy of the enclosed software and are allowed by law to make one backup copy or to copy the contents of the disks onto a single hard disk and keep the originals as your backup or archival copy. United States copyright law prohibits you from making a copy of this software for use on any computer other than your own computer. United States copyright law also prohibits you from copying any written material included in this software package without first obtaining the permission of Adams Media Corporation.

2. Restrictions

You, the end-user, are hereby prohibited from the following:

You may not rent or lease the Software or make copies to rent or lease for profit or for any other purpose.

You may not disassemble or reverse compile for the purposes of reverse engineering the Software.

You may not modify or adapt the Software or documentation in whole or in part, including, but not limited to, translating or creating derivative works.

3. Transfer

You may transfer the Software to another person, provided that (a) you transfer all of the Software and documentation to the same transferee; (b) you do not retain any copies; and (c) the transferee is informed of and agrees to the terms and conditions of this Agreement.

4. Termination

This Agreement and your license to use the Software can be terminated without notice if you fail to comply with any of the provisions set forth in this Agreement. Upon termination of this Agreement, you promise to destroy all copies of the software including backup or archival copies as well as any documentation associated with the Software. All disclaimers of warranties and limitation of liability set forth in this Agreement shall survive any termination of this Agreement.

5. Limited Warranty

Adams Media Corporation warrants that the Software will perform according to the manual and other written materials accompanying the Software for a period of 30 days from the date of receipt. Adams Media Corporation does not accept responsibility for any malfunctioning computer hardware or any incompatibilities with existing or new computer hardware technology.

6. Customer Remedies

Adams Media Corporation's entire liability and your exclusive remedy shall be, at the option of Adams Media Corporation, either refund of your purchase price or repair and/or replacement of Software that does not meet this Limited Warranty. Proof of purchase shall be required. This Limited Warranty will be voided if Software failure was caused by abuse, neglect, accident or misapplication. All replacement Software will be warranted based on the remainder of the warranty or the full 30 days, whichever is shorter and will be subject to the terms of the Agreement.

7. No Other Warranties

ADAMS MEDIA CORPORATION, TO THE FULLEST EXTENT OF THE LAW, DISCLAIMS ALL OTHER WARRANTIES, OTHER THAN THE LIMITED WARRANTY IN PARAGRAPH 5, EITHER EXPRESS OR IMPLIED, ASSOCIATED WITH ITS SOFTWARE, INCLUDING BUT NOT LIMITED TO IMPLIED WARRANTIES OF MERCHANTABILITY AND FITNESS FOR A PARTICULAR PURPOSE, WITH REGARD TO THE SOFTWARE AND ITS ACCOMPANYING WRITTEN MATERIALS. THIS LIMITED WARRANTY GIVES YOU SPECIFIC LEGAL RIGHTS. DEPENDING UPON WHERE THIS SOFTWARE WAS PURCHASED, YOU MAY HAVE OTHER RIGHTS.

8. Limitations on Remedies

TO THE MAXIMUM EXTENT PERMITTED BY LAW, ADAMS MEDIA CORPORATION SHALL NOT BE HELD LIABLE FOR ANY DAMAGES WHATSOEVER, INCLUDING WITHOUT LIMITATION, ANY LOSS FROM PERSONAL INJURY, LOSS OF BUSINESS PROFITS, BUSINESS INTERRUPTION, BUSINESS INFORMATION OR ANY OTHER PECUNIARY LOSS ARISING OUT OF THE USE OF THIS SOFTWARE.

This applies even if Adams Media Corporation has been advised of the possibility of such damages. Adams Media Corporation's entire liability under any provision of this agreement shall be limited to the amount actually paid by you for the Software. Because some states may not allow for this type of limitation of liability, the above limitation may not apply to you.

THE WARRANTY AND REMEDIES SET FORTH ABOVE ARE EXCLUSIVE AND IN LIEU OF ALL OTHERS, ORAL OR WRITTEN, EXPRESS OR IMPLIED. No Adams Media Corporation dealer, distributor, agent, or employee is authorized to make any modification or addition to the warranty.

9. General

This Agreement shall be governed by the laws of the United States of America and the Commonwealth of Massachusetts. If you have any questions concerning this Agreement, contact Adams Media Corporation at 508-427-7100. Or write to us at: Adams Media Corporation, 57 Littlefield Street, Avon, MA 02322.